"I can always count on Donna to give me practical words of wisdom on the things that matter most! She's done it again in *Finding Your Purpose as a Mom*. Chock-full of encouragement on how to create a warm and welcoming environment where God is free to live and do His work, it's a book you won't want to miss!"

—Vickey Banks
Inspirational speaker and author of
Sharing His Secrets and *Love Letters
to My Baby*

"Do you hear God's call, ladies? He is asking us to be 'home-makers.' And He has blessed us with Donna Otto to facilitate that exciting, empowering task. When this book blesses your socks off, be sure you have already taken off your shoes!"

—Kendra Smiley
Helping you LIVE LIFE INTENTION-
ALLY! www.KendraSmiley.com

"*Finding Your Purpose as a Mom* is a must-read! You will be excited and motivated as you read about God's purpose for your life and home."

—Emilie Barnes
author of *Quiet Moments for a Busy Mom's
Soul, Simple Secrets to a Beautiful Home,*
and *If Teacups Could Talk*

"Donna equips and encourages women with godly principles, practical application, and heartwarming stories on the purpose and value of keeping our homes Christ-centered. She doesn't just talk about the importance of home; she lives out those principles within her own life and teaches women how to live it as well. I can't wait to recommend and give this book to women in my life who need her words of wisdom and encouragement on the home front."

—Susan Miller,
author of *After the Boxes Are Unpacked*
and *But Mom, I Don't Want to Move!*

"Donna Otto has written words of wisdom and practical advice for any woman longing to integrate her love for God with her love for home and family. Insightful. Helpful. God-honoring."

—CAROL TRAVILLA,
author of *The Intentional Woman*

"My dear friend Donna Otto loves her God and her home. And what a blessing that she also loves younger women and knows the struggles they have to make their hearts and homes sacred spaces. If that is your struggle too, this book provides the encouragement and practical strategies you've been seeking. After reading it, you and your home will never be the same."

—SANDRA D. WILSON, PH.D.
seminary professor and author of *Released from Shame* and *Into Abba's Arms*

FINDING YOUR PURPOSE as a MOM

DONNA OTTO

with Anne Christian Buchanan

HARVEST HOUSE PUBLISHERS

EUGENE, OREGON

Scripture quotations are taken from the New American Standard Bible®, © 1960, 1962, 1963, 1968, 1971, 1972, 1973, 1975, 1977, 1995 by The Lockman Foundation. Used by permission. (www.Lockman.org)

Cover photo © Bruce Berg Photography

Cover and interior design by Harvest House Publishers, Inc., Eugene, Oregon, Corey Fisher, designer

FINDING YOUR PURPOSE AS A MOM
Copyright © 2004 by Donna Otto with Anne Christian Buchanan
Published by Harvest House Publishers
Eugene, Oregon 97402
www.harvesthousepublishers.com

Library of Congress Cataloging-in-Publication Data

Otto, Donna.
  Finding your purpose as a mom / Donna Otto with Anne Christian Buchanan.
      p. cm.
  Includes bibliographical references.
  ISBN-13: 978-0-7369-1297-6
  ISBN-10: 0-7369-1297-5
  Product # 6912975
  1. Christian women—Religious life. 2. Home—Religious aspects—Christianity. I. Buchanan, Anne Christian. II. Title.
  BV4527.O895 2004
  248.8'431—dc22

                                                                      2004003191

Printed in the United States of America

06   07   08   09   10   / VP-CF /   10   9   8   7   6   5

To Jason and Anissa as they begin
building a home on holy ground.
I love you.

Momma/Mamo

A Homestyle Thank-You

An Italian dinner, served around our dining room table with black-and-white decorations, is planned. There is plenty of food, loads of laughter, and an Otto Dumb Question and apron on the back of every guest's chair. The candles are flickering, the scents are garlic, cheese, and antipasto. The chalkboard at the door says, "Thank you, friends, for all you did to encourage me in this book. May our prayers be answered. Come in."

These are David's and my guests:

Anne Christian Buchanan
Carolyn McCready
LaRae Weikert
Sandy Lane
Bob Hawkins Jr.
Hoppe Household in Oregon
Wayne and Margaret Grudem
Lilies
Kim Moore
Betty Fletcher
Anissa Hamlin
Sandy Wilson
Carol Travilla
Vickey Banks
Kendra Smiley
Emilie and Bob Barnes
Susan Miller
Kay Arthur
Erin Moosbrugger
Homemakers by Choice Board and Staff

Thanks, partner in life, for the privilege of making a home that is holy ground.

CONTENTS

FOREWORD

The Lord has gifted Donna Otto with incredible insight and talent. Her teaching encourages women of all ages (including me) to strive to juggle the responsibilities of being wives, mothers, and grandmothers in addition to the careers and ministry responsibilities the Lord has called us to.

O Beloved, are there times when you're absolutely overwhelmed? The thought of handling it all for another day seems impossible sometimes, doesn't it? I have felt that way many times, and I know from experience how exhausting it can be when there is so much to do and so many people counting on you.

Donna's words are like a breath of fresh air as she consistently conveys nuggets of wisdom that will exhort you to press on in focusing fully on who the Lord has called you to be. Not only is she a talented manager of her own household and priorities, but also she is a gifted communicator. As you read *Finding Your Purpose as a Mom,* I know you will be encouraged as you strive to put into practice the advice Donna has for you. Her experience as a wife and a mother, and her example in pressing on through the hard times, is conveyed beautifully through tips and valuable insights that will benefit us all for a lifetime.

Kay Arthur
CEO and Cofounder
Precept Ministries International

TAKE OFF
YOUR SHOES

WHAT'S THE FIRST THING YOU DO when you enter the house after a long day of running errands or keeping appointments or chasing after your kids—after you put down your purse or the groceries, but before you check the answering machine?

If you're like a lot of women I know, you take off your shoes.

Maybe you want to spare the carpet. Or maybe you're on your way to change into running shoes or hiking boots for a workout. Maybe you can't wait to kick off those pinching pumps and enjoy the luxury of padding around in bare feet...or slip your toes into comfortable house shoes and put up your feet while you nurse the baby or listen to tales of what happened in school that day.

Taking off your shoes—it's such a homey thing to do. It's a thing to do in a place where you feel safe and accepted.

But what does taking off your shoes have to do with finding your purpose as a mom?

More than you might think.

Remember the story of Moses at the burning bush? The young man was in exile from Egypt, the land of his birth, the land where he had learned a painful truth: The people who raised him had enslaved and mistreated the people who gave him life. One day, while alone in the wilderness tending his father-in-law's sheep,

Moses came upon an amazing sight: a burning bush. And as he stared at the bush in wonder, he actually heard God speak:

> "Remove your sandals from your feet, for the place on which you are standing is holy ground" (Exodus 3:5).

God wasn't just telling Moses to get comfortable! He was telling him that something very important was going on, reminding him to show respect and humility in the presence of something sacred. And telling him plainly that the Lord had important work for him to do.

I believe the Lord is speaking a similar word to women today who have the joy and responsibility of tending a home and caring for a family. *Take off your shoes,* he is saying. *The place where you are cooking, cleaning, and raising the next generation is indeed holy ground because you are mine, and your home is part of my plan for changing the world.*

Regardless of who you are, whether you've made the choice to be a stay-at-home mom or work outside the home, whether you are married or single, whether your house is a double-wide in a desert or a mansion on a hillside...I believe this word is for you. Your home really is holy ground because it's a place where God has chosen to live and do his work.

Does thinking about your home that way make you squirm just a little—especially when you think of the piles of laundry in the corner or the dishes in your sink or the way you lost your temper with your children yesterday morning?

I understand your feeling. I've felt it myself. But at the same time, I've come to cherish the understanding that my home and my family are not only God's gifts to me, but a holy trust. They are central to God's purpose for my life—his chosen vehicles for bringing about the future. Home is a place for me to live and to leave a legacy—to build something lasting on holy ground. That reality has been a part of God's plan from the very dawn of creation.

Instead of creating societies with a sweep of his arm, God created a single family—a man and a woman. He gave them a home, a special place to live and to be. He gave them responsibility for populating the earth and caring for the rest of creation—with specific roles for each of them. And even after they disobeyed him and had to leave the garden that was their first dwelling, the new homes they established continued to be significant in God's plan of redemption.

Throughout the Old and New Testaments we find the idea that homes are places where souls are nourished and where God's ways are taught. A few passages, like Deuteronomy 6:4-9, state this specifically. Some, like Proverbs 31 and passages from Paul, elaborate on the roles and responsibilities of men and women and children in the home. And many others take as a given that God's work in a human life begins at home, around a hearth, in loving relationship to a family that lives and works and worships together. In fact, the Bible refers to houses, homes, and dwelling places more than 600 times.

Home matters to God, in other words, and it should matter to you. It's at the heart of who you are as a mom and as a person.

Surely it's important to remember that when God sent his Son into the world, he chose to place him in the setting of a home and family, a warm place where he could grow in wisdom and stature and favor with God and man. After Jesus embarked on his ministry, though he himself didn't have a specific place "to lay His head" (Matthew 8:20), he obviously treasured the homes opened to him. And although he called his disciples away from their homes and sometimes, for emphasis, seemed to urge them to break their family ties, a look behind the scenes shows his tender regard for home and family. Why else would he have bothered to work miracles at a wedding, heal Peter's mother-in-law, and make arrangements, while in agony on the cross, for the care of his aging mother?

From the very beginning, God has made it clear: Home is holy ground. *Your* home is holy ground. And it's your privilege and your responsibility, even amid the messes and confusion of daily life, not only to take off your shoes, but to tend the holy flame. As a human being in whom God's Spirit dwells, you have that privilege. As a woman and as a mother, you have a special set of gifts and responsibilities. You are called to create and maintain a home environment and atmosphere that reflects God's love, God's hope, God's peace—quite literally, to build your home on holy ground.

In my years as a wife, mother, homemaker, and teacher, I've picked up some ideas about how this can be done. I've shared these over the years through the organization Homemakers by Choice, which I founded as a support group for women who have a heart for their homes. In this book, I'd like to share them with you as well.

But this is a handbook, not an all-comprehensive guide. It's not designed to tell you everything you need to know about caring for your children or maintaining your home. Instead, I want to help you make heart-deep decisions about who you are in relation to your home and family...and who God wants you to be. How you use this will depend on your circumstances—your stage in life, your marital status, your work situation. Whoever you are, I hope *Finding Your Purpose as a Mom* will encourage you, give you strength, help you see the big picture, and understand better what it means to be a mother after God's own heart.

I've written several books about practical ideas you can use in your home—organizational hints, decorating suggestions, and so on. There will be practical material in this book as well. But the heart of what I want to share with you is not *what to do* but *who you are* and *how you think.* I want to encourage you to think about how you relate to your home base, this place where you sleep, wash, pray, train your children, and, yes, take off your shoes.

I want to affirm for you the heavenly importance of what you do in your home—whether it's scrubbing toilets or cooking dinner or playing Monopoly with a house full of children, and whether you do it full-time or in conjunction with outside work. I hope I can sway you to think both *intentionally* and *counterculturally* about what it means to be the mood setter in your house.

Intentional thinking is important because I think much of our culture has fallen into the assumption that home will just take care of itself. Women used to know better, but I find that many women today are completely unaware that shaping a nurturing home environment, like any other important endeavor, takes planning, purpose, organization, and time. If we want our homes to be warm and welcoming and to be successful at raising saints for the King, we need to arrange for that to happen. We need to do it on purpose.

And I think that *countercultural* thinking is absolutely crucial because our current American culture tends to be absolutely clueless and perverse in the way it views home life and motherhood. We live in a society that features entire cable channels about "house beautiful," whetting our appetites for homemade bread (with homegrown herbs!) and crisp, fragrant hand-embroidered sheets—yet seems to assume we can do it all in just a few hours in the evenings after a hard day at the office. It's a culture that assumes a home can be broken up at will, regardless of the consequences, and that everybody will "adjust" just fine. It's a culture that glorifies "nurturing children"…and deeply distrusts people who choose to make nurturing their entire career.

As followers of Christ, no matter what our specific circumstances or our personal decisions, I believe we need to take a stand against this schizophrenic culture that both idolizes and devalues home life. We need to move beyond house beautiful and house status and house drudgery into the heavenly reality of house holy.

Take off your shoes, because your home can be a gift of safety and comfort and freedom for you and your family. Because something sacred can happen there—in fact, it's *supposed* to happen there. Your precious Savior wants to use your life and your work and your role as a mom to change the world.

Take off your shoes. And then you might want to roll up your sleeves. The challenging and fulfilling task of being a purposeful mom in a holy home awaits you.

Donna Otto
Scottsdale, Arizona

WHAT IS A HOME?

*H*ome can be...

an arcade, a theater, a museum, an office, a classroom,
a laundry, a restaurant, a garden center or workshop
a storage unit or hotel
or even a battleground.

Home can be all these things—in part.
But none of these things are the essence of home.

Home is a place of shelter, safe and warm.
It's a growing place, a teaching institution, first church, and seminary.
Home is a hospitality center, a mission field.
It's a base for traditions and memories,
A place to return to with joy.

Home is a place where God lives.
This home—your home—is holy ground.

Take off your shoes.

DONNA OTTO

PART ONE

It Begins
with You

~·~

*And Mary said, "...may it be done to me
according to your word."*

LUKE 1:38

ONE

YOU ARE
HOLY GROUND

The year was 1945, and the young newlyweds had a dream: They would build a house together. They found a small piece of property with a narrow but wonderful view of Puget Sound and planned their dream house. The dream was for a modest home with a two-car garage—an extravagant vision for that day when housing was scarce. But the plan was to work on the dream a little a time. So they began. They bought the lot and saved for the house. They built the garage first and then, in order to save money, moved into it, partitioning the space into small rooms.

Some 55 years later, the now-widowed wife was still living in that little converted garage. For a variety of reasons, the dream house had never materialized, and trees had gradually obscured the view. Yet, as neighbors and relatives will tell you, that small space had served well the family that was raised there. And to the daughters and grandchildren who traveled back often to visit, that tiny converted garage always felt like a haven of love.

Later, at the mother's funeral, the two daughters marveled at how warm and alive that little garage-house had seemed during their growing years. Without the presence of their mother, the little space looked tiny and incomplete. With her, it had radiated joy, faith, energy, and warmth. There they received large portions of encouragement, grace, and beauty. That converted garage had never seemed small to them. It always felt as spacious and embracing as the love that lived there. The space their mother had made so special always felt—well, like home.

Home. It's a beautiful word to most of us. It sounds like comfort, acceptance, relaxation, and love. It sounds like a warm place to be, a good place to grow up. Like a place where most of us would love to live, even if we've never had that kind of home before.

Our culture, in some ways, seems to be obsessed with the idea of home, especially in the early years of the twenty-first century. At the same time, most of us would admit that the institution of the home is in trouble. The fallout from dysfunctional and broken families litters the landscape. To our culture, home is often a status symbol, a way of showing off (or of judging others). It is sometimes a hiding place, a way of isolating ourselves from everyone else. And for many home is a source of inner conflict as our yearning for fireside comforts clashes with our ambitions and outside interests.

As believers, I believe we are called to see our earthly homes as something completely different. We are called to look at our homes the way God sees them—as vital centers for accomplishing his work on earth. Homes are tangible places where his love, mercy, and righteousness are taught and practiced on a regular basis. In a sense, a home is an incarnation center—a place where important attributes of God become real in the material world.

Think about it. Our homes are a refuge, just as the Lord is our refuge. Our homes give us comfort and strength and serve as tangible reminders of the God who is the Source of all comfort and strength. In our homes we can experience beauty and stillness and hilarious joy, just as we serve the God of all beauty and stillness and joy. And just as God is relationship in his very triune nature—Father, Son, and Holy Spirit—home is where our deepest, most meaningful relationships can flourish.

Ideally, in other words, whatever is good about God should actually be fleshed out in the physical spaces of a believing home, just as it is lived out in the lives of individual believers. When we share our homes with others, we are extending the grace of God to them. When we teach our children and love our husbands, we are helping them grow in truth and understand the depths of the Father's love. Even when we take off our shoes to relax, we are in the presence of God's awesome and lovely reality.

And yes, I know that's a difficult proposition—because homes are also places where sinners live. And that means our homes, like our lives in general, will always be in need of some sprucing up. Sometimes they scream out for a complete remodeling job! Our homes, like our lives, will always be in the process of becoming what God wants them to be. And our homes here on earth, remember, just like our bodies, will never be more than temporary dwelling places anyway. As the old gospel songs remind us, this earth is not really our home.

And yet this earth is the place where God has chosen to make himself known. He has given you an earthly body, an earthly home in which to dwell, an earthly life in which to grow and learn and make a difference, an earthly family to raise and nurture. And if you have made the choice to follow Christ, Christ has promised to dwell with you. Which is why it's not just your home that's holy ground.

You yourself are holy ground.

And that's exactly where the act of shaping your home and finding your purpose as a mom begins—with you. With the woman you are and the woman who, with God's help, you can become.

You may be like me and come from a barren background, one without affirmation, joy, or safety. And you may have fallen short in your desire to create and maintain a wholesome, godly environment for yourself and your family. But wherever you are, that is not where you need to remain.

Within the family of God, you can establish a home environment that is anything but barren, one rich with tradition, encouragement, and personal growth. Your home can be a place where wonderful memories are created that will resonate across generations, a place where each person lives for the other and all live for God. Your home can be a taste of heaven on earth—a foretaste of heaven for everyone who lives there.

And where do you start that amazing adventure?

You start with you. And you start by saying yes.

A Moment of REFLECTION

1. When you see the word "home," what pictures spring into your mind? What does this tell you about yourself?

2. What does it mean to think of *yourself* as holy ground? Is this hard for you to imagine?

3. What does the word "homemaker" mean to you? Can you relate to the word, or does it seem foreign and scary? What word would you use to describe the important task of creating and maintaining a godly home environment?

THE BEAUTY OF A HOME

The beauty of a home is order.
The blessing of a home is contentment.
The glory of a home is hospitality.
The crown of a home is godliness.

SOURCE UNKNOWN

TWO

STARTING WITH YES

I FIND IT INTERESTING THAT THE STORY ABOUT how Jesus came to have his first earthly home began with an individual visit to an individual woman. And talk about a change of plans. What happened in that simple exchange between the angel and Mary changed the course of history!

Mary surely had dreamed about what her life would be like as a woman. Like most young girls—like you, probably—she had visions of how she would decorate her house, what special touches she would add, how she would use her particular skills to make a home for her family. As a betrothed young woman, she probably daydreamed about what married life would be like, how she and Joseph would get along, how many children they would have, what it would be like to be a mother. Perhaps she wondered how she would get along with her mother-in-law.

Certainly, as a well-trained Hebrew girl living under Roman rule, Mary knew what was expected of her. She had practiced homemaking skills since she was a child—fetching water, baking bread, weaving cloth. She had heard the words of Proverbs 31. She had every reason to expect a respectable and fulfilling home life. But of all the things Mary dreamed about her future, surely it never occurred to her that God himself had plans to change the world through her body and her home. It never crossed her mind that her dream home would also be ground zero for the Messiah's coming, the incarnation of God's own Son.

Even when the angel brought her the message, Mary had trouble getting her mind around it. At first she couldn't even speak. And when she did, the first words out of her mouth were, "How can this be?"

What the angel was telling Mary about herself and her future home wasn't at all what she had imagined in all those daydreams. It was so much better and deeper, so much more wonderful. This young woman was blessed to play a key role in the most important drama of all human history—once she said yes to what God had in mind.

That's the first thing to remember when you think about finding your purpose as a mom and living on the holy ground of your home. How it all turns out will probably surprise you. But there's something even more important that we can learn from Mary's story.

The first thing the angel said when he approached Mary was not: "All right, this is what is going to happen…" He didn't outline the plan right away or hand her an organizer or a paintbrush or even a set of swaddling clothes. Instead, the first thing he did was to speak directly to Mary as a woman: "Greetings, favored one! The Lord is with you" (Luke 1:28).

And this, I believe, is where God always starts: with who we are as women. It's where he wants to start with you in this worthy calling of shaping a home environment that honors him. Before you ever get around to organizing and planning and disciplining and decorating, even before you ponder details of your role as a shaper of your home environment—you need to begin where he begins, with his call to you as a woman.

Making a home, to put it simply, begins with you. Not because you're the center of the universe, but because any change in your environment has to begin with the woman you are. It must begin with your understanding of who you are as a woman of God, with your vision for what he wants your life to be and your plan for making that vision a reality.

God has gifted you with the ability and the responsibility to shape your home to his glory. And this is true no matter what your circumstances are—whether you're married or single, employed outside the home or not, surrounded by children or looking forward someday to a family of your own. And it's true whether you are a mature, insightful woman who has made all the right choices or you are looking around at the ruins of your own home life and wondering how in the world you can ever get there from here.

OTTO'S MOTTO

It all starts with the Big Yes.

So how do you begin with you?

You begin where Mary began—by saying yes. You begin by being willing to open your heart to the working of the Holy Spirit. You begin by giving God permission to be in charge, even if the person and the place where you end up weren't what you dreamed of all along. More specifically, you say yes to what God is going to do with the woman you are in your own home and with your own family. You open your home to him, just as you opened your heart.

That's what Mary did, once she began to understand what was happening to her. Though the angel had just turned her daydreams inside out and stretched her mind with a promise that would require much of her, she was willing to participate: "Behold, the bondslave of the Lord; may it be done to me according to your word" (Luke 1:38).

Now, this yes was obviously not the first yes Mary had ever said to the Lord. She was already a woman of God from a good Jewish family and well taught in the ways of the Lord. Somewhere along the road, no doubt, consciously or unconsciously, she had said what I call the "Big Yes" and allowed God into her life. This particular yes, the one she gave to the angel, was all about her family and her home and her future. She was, in a sense, inviting God into her home and giving him permission to rearrange things any way he wanted. And that's the yes I believe we all need to make at some point in our lives. It's the yes that recognizes that our homes are holy ground.

But here's something else to keep in mind. Once Mary had said yes to the angel, as far as I can tell, she kept on saying yes to what God was doing in her life and her home. We aren't told that directly, but it's clear from biblical accounts. She said: "Yes, I'll go to Bethlehem with my husband, even though I'm very pregnant." She said, "Yes, I'll settle for a stable," and "Yes, I'll agree to let all those grungy shepherds in to see my newborn." Much later she said, "Yes, I'll let my Son leave home to be an itinerant preacher." And, "Yes, no matter what, I'll be there with him—even at the foot of a cross."

The life of Mary shows that great things, important things, always begin with someone saying yes to God, and then they move along one yes at a time. When you keep in mind that your whole life is holy ground, you keep yourself open to the wonderful opportunities he has planned for you.

This means, of course, that there will be surprises, maybe big ones. You may find yourself in circumstances vastly different from what you always imagined. Perhaps you always fancied yourself as a sophisticated city loft dweller and will end up in a comfortable, child-friendly suburban home...or a sleek, stylish mansion...or a double-wide mobile home. Quite possibly your dreams for your marriage and your children will turn out different from what you planned—but this is true no matter what your choices or your attitude. None of us can predict the course of our lives, but we can choose to put our lives in the hands of the One who knows our end from our beginning.

There will be sacrifices as well as surprises when you say yes to God—sacrifices of your time, of your plans, and sometimes of your dearly held dreams. The job of raising your children in a God-centered home can be both physically and emotionally strenuous. Establishing an intentional, countercultural home will probably mean giving up some of your personal desires. Even as a physical reality, homes are high-maintenance items, and that is true of the emotional and spiritual aspects of homekeeping as well. That's why you'll find one yes leads to another—and some yeses are a lot easier to say than others.

But keep in mind that God's intention overall is to bless you—in your life as a woman, and in your life at home. He has already blessed you. You are truly his beloved, and he wants you to take that to heart before you ever pick up a paintbrush. He has prepared for you a home in heaven that far surpasses any home you can create here on earth. He has promised to dwell in you just as you dwell in him. And he has indeed favored you among women by giving you a vital part in the process of bringing about his kingdom on earth.

Once you say yes to the Lord, you won't know exactly where you will end up, but you can know you'll always find your way home.

A Moment of REFLECTION

1. Can you remember the first time you consciously said yes to God in your life?

2. Have you specifically said yes to God in regard to your home and your family?

3. What are some of the fears you have of ways that God may change your life if you say yes to him?

What God Thinks of You
(A SCRIPTURAL SAMPLER)

It all begins with you—with your answer to God's call on your life. So it helps to get an idea what God thinks of you. He tells you clearly in the words of Scripture.

- *He loves you with an everlasting love (Jeremiah 31:3; John 3:16).*

- *He created you in his image (Genesis 1:27).*

- *You are his child (John 1:12; Romans 8:16; Ephesians 1:5).*

- *He knows you intimately and by name (Isaiah 43:1; Matthew 10:30; John 10:3).*

- *He made you exactly the way he wanted (Psalm 139:13-18).*

- *He cared enough to give his only Son to redeem you from your sins (John 3:16).*

- *You are a new creation in him (2 Corinthians 5:17; Ephesians 5:8; Colossians 2:13).*

- *He wants you to trust him to take care of you (1 Peter 5:7).*

- *If you have children, he has a specific set of responsibilities for you (Proverbs 22:6; Proverbs 23:13-14; Colossians 3).*

THREE

STARTING FROM
WHERE YOU ARE

I DON'T KNOW WHERE YOU ARE in your spiritual life. I don't know what your home life is like or even what you want it to be. But I do know that if you begin by saying yes to what the Lord has in mind for you and your home, he will begin to move you toward being the woman he wants you to be. And he will begin opening your eyes to a vision of what your home could be as well.

I'm thinking particularly about a young couple I know who started life together with all the odds against them. They married because she was pregnant with his child. And from the beginning that home and that marriage were a nightmare. Both parents were young and immature. They fought constantly, and the police visited their home more often than the family did.

Eventually, after five years of marriage, this young man and woman separated. She took their young child and went to live with her parents. And it was during this time of separation that she finally said yes to God's calling for herself and her home. Now, you have to understand exactly how things stood for this young woman when she did this. She didn't even *have* a home at the time. She was living apart from her husband, who had absolutely no interest in spiritual things and no use for God. Between the two of them loomed a mountain of baggage—painful memories, regrets, distrust, and disagreement.

But still that young woman said yes. She said, "This is about me and about God. And I choose to believe that God can somehow redeem what has gone before: my sleeping with this man and getting pregnant, and the five years of misery and the police. I will do everything I can to make and keep a holy home." She said yes to God's call on her as a woman, wife, mother, and homemaker. And then she set to work doing...nothing. Nothing, that is, except to pray and read her Bible. She developed a commitment to spending time in the Word. She asked a little group of young women to pray with her. And week after week, they prayed a single, focused prayer that her husband would come to Christ.

Very gradually, over a period of time, hope began to enter that young couple's relationship. The wife began to change, and her husband was drawn to the new person she was becoming. He asked her out, and they began to see each other. Then he realized he wanted to be in the marriage with her and be a father to their child. So they moved back in together, and she continued to pray. She prayed for two years, very faithfully, with her little band of friends.

OTTO'S MOTTO

Finish strong.
Remember: the common start,
the uncommon finish.

Finally it happened. The husband gloriously came to Christ. He told his wife, "I've thought about this for a year, and I've looked at that little four spiritual laws book, and finally I think it's about me." From that point, that woman and man began to build a holy home.

It hasn't been an easy process. This couple still lags behind many of their peers in emotional, spiritual, and marital commitment. Their baggage of pain and resentment is still being cleared out, and they are having to learn completely new ways of being together. They've been in counseling a lot. Still, the difference is amazing. Holy things are happening in that household, and it all began when a young woman, against all odds, said yes to what God could do in her home.

Now the truth is—as that young woman will no doubt agree—it's really better not to do it the way she did. It's truly important to make wise choices about who you are and who you will marry and what kind of home you plan to establish. Basic homemaking skills—preferably learned in childhood and practiced over the years—are a big plus. And spending time in the Word and in prayer and establishing yourself as a woman of God *before* you ever take the step to become a mom and establish a home is by far the better choice.

But the truth also is that you can say yes anytime. You can say yes as the person you are, and God will take you from there.

The outcome may not be exactly what it was with the young couple I just described. You know as well as I do that not all broken marriages are reconciled, not every mistake so directly redeemed. Yet God is faithful, and I can guarantee that saying yes to his plan for your home will never be pointless or fruitless.

Because you are his child, you are already blessed among women. As you say yes to him—and yes and yes and yes—he will take it from there. He will give you the vision and direction you need to be the kind of mom—and woman—you need to be so that you can make your home into a beautiful, fruitful, holy place.

A Moment of
REFLECTION

1. What are some of the mistakes you've made in your home life—or your life in general—that you regret?

2. What kind of life choices make it easier to say yes to the Lord?

SETTING THE THERMOSTAT FOR PEACE

- ❧ *Make peace at home a priority.*
- ❧ *Practice trust and gratitude.*
- ❧ *Live with a thankful heart.*
- ❧ *Cultivate a quiet heart—give yourself the peace you need.*
- ❧ *Cultivate a gentle spirit.*
- ❧ *Learn to speak softly.*
- ❧ *Know your family.*
- ❧ *Cultivate a spirit of "we."*
- ❧ *Provide peaceful places for those you love.*

FOUR

THE PICTURE ON THE FRONT OF THE PUZZLE BOX

CREATING AND KEEPING A HOME THAT REFLECTS God and his creation requires choices. That's what we've really been talking about when we talk about saying yes. Yes is a choice. And choices make a big difference in our lives.

The most courageous, life-changing choice you will ever make is to say yes to Jesus. When the Holy Spirit brings us to the place where we see the need for Jesus as Lord in our life, we bend our hearts and minds, not to mention our knees, and say the Big Yes. But life is full of so many other choices, including the specific ones you make that will affect the quality of your life and home. The choice of whether you will marry—and especially *whom* you will marry—is a big choice that directly influences the environment where you live. So do your choices of location (city or suburb, house or apartment, rent, buy, or build), how big your family will be (how many children, timing, infertility issues), and how you will handle issues of income and career (full-time job, part-time job, stay-at-home mom). Every day you continue to make little and large choices that shape the atmosphere of your home.

What's the key to making wise choices in these matters? You probably already have a list of good answers: Search the Scriptures, ask for wise counsel, make lists of pros and cons, write out goals, and make plans. All these approaches are appropriate and helpful. I absolutely recommend them...but not first.

In my opinion, the first and most valuable step you should make after saying yes to God's call, the absolute key to finding your purpose as a mom, is to get a clear picture in your head of what you are trying to accomplish.

I'm not talking about your goals. I'm talking about your vision, about the picture you hold in your head of what a holy, God-centered home can be. Why is this important? Because to do anything, you first have to envision it.

Yet even as I write that, I know it's not completely true. Much of the Lord's work through the centuries has been done by men and women who blunder through life one tiny idea at a time. Even when we don't have a clear vision of where we're going, we can still be obedient, and God will lead us where he wants us to go.

Still, it's easier to get where you're going when you have a mental picture of what you're striving for. It's like working a jigsaw puzzle—it goes faster when you can look at the picture on the box. The process of shaping a warm, loving, nurturing home becomes a lot easier when you already have an idea what such a home would be like.

Where do you find such a picture? To a certain extent, you already carry it in your heart. It's a composite of every happy home you've ever experienced, every homesick longing you've ever felt in the pit of your stomach. It's created out of need, but I believe that need is related to the essential homesickness God has built into every human soul. Deep in our hearts, we have a picture of what a perfect, holy home would be like because our Creator made us to yearn for such a place.

Years ago, when I was invited to become involved with a home-based sales organization, our "team leader" led us in an exercise I remember to this day. He gave us scissors and a stack of magazines and asked us to cut out pictures we liked. The idea was to collect images of cars, appliances, and jewelry—desirable objects our successful sales would allow us to obtain. Our leader urged us to paste our pictures on a piece of poster board and hang them in a prominent place in our homes to motivate our work.

As I sat there with scissors in my hand, I suddenly realized I had been doing this kind of exercise all my life in my mind. Even as a child in a cold, uncomfortable environment, I filled my mind with pictures of what a wonderful, calm, caring home would look like. I knew what kind of furniture it would have, how it would be decorated, what people would do there, how people would be treated. I envisioned a pretty home, a warm place that made others feel welcome, a fun place for people to gather. I pictured a loving husband and lively children—six of them, in fact.

I didn't know how to find a home like that, and I certainly didn't know how to go about creating one, but I knew what I yearned for. In a sense, that picture in my heart kept my hope alive and motivated me to learn. After I married my husband, David, and our daughter, Anissa, was born, this picture helped me make important choices that shaped our lives. Granted, I had to adjust my vision a bit over the years to make room for David and Anissa's ideas and conform to my growing understanding of what God wanted in my life. (Those other five children never did materialize.) But still, it's hard to overestimate how much the pictures in my mind have helped me achieve the kind of life I yearned for.

I realized this anew in the months when I was finishing this book and our Anissa was preparing to be married. Since the day she was born, and even before, I have envisioned her wedding day. I pictured the parties, the intimate moments, the shared love. I dreamed of the way I wanted to act, what I hoped this family event would represent. I saw Anissa's future wedding as an affirmation of our shared faith, a gathering of beloved friends, a time of maximum celebration and minimum tension. And that's what it turned out to be! Our Anissa's wedding day beautifully reflected her and Jason's unique personalities, but our family celebration was also shaped by the pictures that have filled my heart and mind for so many years.

The picture in your heart is a good starting place for shaping your home. Just close your eyes and visualize your home the way it could be—a home whose ambience and activities reflect the holy place it really is. Picture yourself walking up to the door, unlocking it, and stepping inside. You're home...

Your front door swings open to a place that is both lively and serene. You step into the most wonderful, comfortable house you can imagine. The colors are delicious—the kinds of colors that always make you feel happy and relaxed. The furniture is both visually pleasing and inviting—you want to sink into one of those chairs. The floors are cool and smooth, the carpets soothing to your feet. Dappled light streams in from spacious, tree-shaded windows.

It's clear this house is also well kept. You see that in the weed-less gardens; you feel it in the nonsticky floors. It's peaceful too— organized and calm. But it's far from a showplace home; it's a house people actually live in. You see that in clusters of family photos, stacks of books, soup on the stove, a scribbled-on pad next to the telephone, and newspapers next to a chair.

Clearly, something good is going on here. This place feels friendly, even fun. You hear children's voices or the buzz of adults talking together. There's an apron on a hook in the kitchen, a craft project in progress in the den, an open Bible on a desk. The message light blinks on the answering machine. Though a sense of order pervades the house, the place is anything but sterile.

Do you see what I mean? If you can imagine a home that feels like that—not necessarily the details, but the atmosphere—you'll be a lot closer to making it happen.

Picture it vividly enough, and you'll find it a lot easier to make it real.

Envision it well, and then you can start to choose.

A Moment of
REFLECTION

1. Use the diagram on page 40 to help you visualize what you want your home to be. What kind of people, conversations, and priorities do you want to fill your home life? Write in phrases, draw pictures—whatever helps you capture your vision. (The pictures and words surrounding the diagram will give you some ideas.)

2. On a separate page, write a description of what your current home situation is like. If possible, do this on a different day. Try to isolate a single act you can do today to make your current home better resemble your visualized home.

A Vision of Home

FIVE

YOUR HEAVENLY HOME

Let's go one step further with this idea of envisioning what your home could be like. After all, we're not talking about magical thinking—making a wish and hoping it will come true. And we're not just talking about shopping for lamps and fabric to capture a certain ambience. We're talking about catching *God's* vision for your home and your life as a mom. And yes, that vision comes partly from the imagination God has given you and the dreams and yearnings he has built into your soul. But a vision for your home isn't just about your desires, and it's not something you need to dream up out of thin air. The picture is already drawn for you, right there in the Bible. God gives us an unmistakable picture of what such a home is like when he tells us what our *real* home is like.

I'm talking about heaven.

After all, the Bible makes it clear that this earth is not our ultimate dwelling place. Our real home is with the Lord, in the place he has prepared for us. The most wonderful, godly home here on earth is a poor imitation of the wonderful place in which we will eventually dwell. Still, I believe we will come closer to God's ideal for our homes when we model them after what we know of heaven.

In fact, I'm convinced it's the reason God gives us homes in the first place. They are not intended just to be operation centers, not just places to eat or sleep. Instead, they are places that give us all a sense of what life with the Father can be like, a taste for the eternal. Charles Parkhurst put it this way: "Home interprets heaven. Home is heaven for beginners."

To get a clear vision for what your home can be, then, consider what the Bible says about what Christ's future millennial kingdom and heaven are like. We find such descriptions in Psalm 46, for example, and in Isaiah 11 and 65 and in the book of Revelation, as well as in some of the words of Jesus. And these word pictures, I believe, provide a useful model for living on holy ground right now on earth.

One of the first things we learn about our eternal home in the Bible, for instance, is that it's *a place of beauty*, a delight to the senses. The popular images of angels killing time on featureless clouds don't even come close to the gorgeous images we are given in the Bible about our future home. Instead, the Bible describes both crafted beauty (jeweled thrones, golden and marble structures) and natural beauty (flowing rivers, beautiful trees, soaring mountains).

Now, chances are you don't have a chance of living in a bejeweled, golden palace. You probably don't have (or want) rivers flowing through your home. You might not even enjoy a decent view. But that basic principle of beauty can still begin to shape a vision of what your home could be. To the best of your ability, it should be a place that looks good (colors, shapes, arrangement), smells good (candles, potpourri), feels good to the touch (upholstery, carpets, and flooring), and even tastes good (what's in the kitchen?). There should be a place for lovely man-made items (your bell collection, a sampler from a friend) as well as a touch of the outdoors (a potted plant, a piece of driftwood). Anything that reminds you of God's beautiful handiwork will help you keep your vision on the beauty of your heavenly home.

But heaven of course, is more than beautiful. It is also *a place of peace, safety, comfort, and belonging.* This a place where pain is absent, where there is no fear—in fact, the zoo gates will be opened wide and lions and lambs and little children will all play together. The sun doesn't burn too hot by day, and danger never lurks in the shadows at night.

Oh, that our homes could offer that kind of safety and comfort to those who enter! Because we still live in a fallen world, we don't have the power to offer such absolute freedom from fear and discomfort. (Sometimes, in the interest of training our children, we even need to *cause* some discomfort.) But we can still strive toward establishing homes that are as safe and comforting as we can make them. At the very least, that means a home free from known safety hazards. It means a place as physically comfortable as possible—not too hot, not too cold, with furniture that fits the frames of those who need to sit and fabrics that welcome family and visitors alike. And even more important, a home that gives a foretaste of heaven is a home that is *emotionally* safe, where each person's dignity and feelings are protected.

In a safe and comforting house, family members listen to each other and build one another up. Children are helped and protected and taught how to live. Adults are respected and supported and given shelter from the stresses of "making it" in the world. Everyone is nurtured and encouraged. That's the kind of home that shows clearly what heaven is like—truly a place where "God will wipe every tear" (Revelation 7:17).

What else do we know about heaven that can serve as a model for our earthly homes? We know it will be *a gathering place*, a place of communion with God and others. The Bible does not tell us definitively whether our earthly relationships will survive intact, but it does make pretty clear that we will *have* relationships. We see that from the biblical descriptions of feasting and celebration, of crowds thronging together to praise the Lord. Heaven will quite clearly be a place where the Lord's people gather. There will be singing. There will be talking. There will be a wonderful and joyful sense of being together, surrounded by love.

And this is a wonderful picture, too, of a "heavenly" home here on earth. It's a place where people love to be together. There is plenty of joyful interaction—and not just sitting side by side in front of the tube. People like to gather there for warm hugs, quiet conversation, fun and games, shared meals. There will also be shared work projects and shared responsibilities.

Home, like heaven, is a place where family members and guests alike make time to really *know* each other, to share their hearts and their lives. And they do this in an atmosphere of calm, not chaos, because a heavenlike home is almost certainly *an orderly place.* The biblical images clearly show God's realm as a place of order and organization. The chain of authority is clear—God is above all, with Christ on his right hand and everyone else arranged accordingly. People know where to go, where they belong. But it's important to recognize that the organizing principles in all of this is love, not just arbitrary power. Behind all the beauty and celebration is a serene but energetic sense of order, a comforting sense that everything is as it should be, that the center is holding even while miracles unfold.

Doesn't that describe a home where you would like to live? A heavenlike home needs to be organized so that important details don't fall through the cracks and clutter and emergencies don't detract from what is truly important. The energetic order that God has built into the very universe is echoed in the lively but smooth running of a household. But this order, too, is characterized and ruled by care and concern for one another. Organization in this kind of home is a loving tool, never a power trip.

It almost goes without saying that heaven will be *a place of truth,* a place where the secrets of the universe will be revealed: "For now we see in a mirror dimly," writes the apostle Paul in 1 Corinthians 13:12, "but then face to face." It follows that an earthly home after God's own heart will be one that honors the truth and steers others toward understanding. It's a place of learning, in other words—a place for active minds, for questioning and discussing, for learning from one another. It's a place for loving honesty, a place where we can learn about ourselves by revealing ourselves as we really are. And, of course, it's a place that honors God's truth as well, where his Word is read and respected.

Heaven is also *a welcoming, hospitable place.* That's part of the picture Jesus draws for us when he says, "In my Father's house are many dwelling places…I go to prepare a place for you" (John 14:2). A special place, prepared just for us—what a picture of welcome! We also have Jesus' image of a Father opening his arms for the prodigal son, welcoming his own child home with redeeming love. We even have his direct and welcoming invitation: "Come to Me, all who are weary and heavy-laden, and I will give you rest" (Matthew 11:28).

What does a welcoming home here on earth look like? You know it if you've ever experienced it! It's a place of open arms and open hearts, where guests are treated like family and family are treated like special guests, where faces smile a greeting and hands work hard to make things ready. There is always a little something set aside for visitors—a snack in the freezer, some space in a closet, an extra place at the table. The house is kept reasonably clean and ready, and the heart is kept open enough to welcome company even if the house *isn't* completely clean.

A final point to remember about our heavenly home is that it *is a place where God is present and God rules.* Isn't this the very definition of heaven? Biblical descriptions of the heavenly city, the holy mountain, the kingdom of God all focus on the central reality that God is there. Worship and praise are primary activities. And because God is present and God is love, our heavenly home will be above all a place of unending and overwhelming love and goodness: "The lovingkindness of the LORD is from everlasting to everlasting on those who fear Him, and His righteousness to children's children" (Psalm 103:17).

The truth is that we will never experience that kind of perfection in our lives on earth. But if our homes and our lives don't clearly reflect the Lord's presence, we can know that something is wrong. After all, he has promised to dwell in us and with us. He has promised to come into our lives when we answer his knock on our door.

I don't know about you, but I want anyone who walks in my door and everyone who shares my home with me to receive a sense that the Lord is present. I want everything about my home, from the décor to the conversation to the activities, to reveal God's love and to inspire a response of worship and praise.

For even though my home will not last forever, the souls who live here and visit here certainly will. I pray that the love they experience here will be enough to give them a little taste of heaven, a picture of what their life in Christ can be...from everlasting to everlasting.

Surely that is the heart of my purpose as a mom.

A Moment of REFLECTION

1. Compare your current home description with both your "dream home" and the description of a heavenly home. What elements in your current situation conform to your dreams and the Bible's description? Which are different?

2. Choose one point of discrepancy between a "heavenly home" and your current home. Write down three ideas for how you can make improvements in this area.

THE ONE-MINUTE MEZUZAH

*B*ecause we human beings tend to be fickle and forgetful, it helps to develop a system to remind us about our choices. The Jewish people have a tradition designed to do just that. On the right side of every Jewish doorpost is a small container called a "mezuzah" that holds a key passage from Deuteronomy 6 called the Shema (Deuteronomy 6:4-9). The mezuzah is a visual symbol marking the house as holy ground; it serves to remind visitors and inhabitants alike that the people in this household have said yes to God. Here are some other very quick ways of adding reminders around your household:

- Borrow your kids' chalk and write: "This house belongs to God" over the front door on the inside. Or get really brave and paint it on!

- "As for me and my house, we will serve the LORD" (Joshua 24:15). Write the Scripture out on an index card and post it on your refrigerator or bulletin board.

- Find an inexpensive plaque showing a spiritual symbol that has particular meaning to you—a cross, a fish, an angel—and hang it on your bedroom wall where you can see it first thing in the morning and last thing at night.

- Take a hint from my dear friend Emilie Barnes: Gather your devotional materials into a beautiful basket and leave it in a convenient spot.

—⊂ SIX ⊃—

HELP!

IF YOUR HOME IS ALREADY THE SLICE OF heaven on earth I've just described—a warm, welcoming, and worshipful place where people live in harmony, guests feel right at home, and God is always honored—chances are you don't even need this book. But I doubt that is true, because only in heaven itself will we experience that kind of perfect home. Here on earth, we can all use a little help...or a lot!

The wonderful news is that help is available. God never asks anything of us without giving us what we need to do it, and that's true of the task of making and keeping earthly homes that honor him. If you say yes to the Lord's calling to make your home holy ground, he will provide you with an adequate support system to make it happen. Now, the kind of support God offers is not likely to arrive in the form of a maid standing on your doorstep, all expenses paid. (At this point you're allowed a big sigh!) It probably won't take the form of a new, helpful friend appearing in your life out of the blue, although that has actually happened to me. Only rarely will it involve clear, direct marching orders from the Lord—although this, too, happens from time to time.

Even Mary, as far as we know, didn't have specific daily instruction from an angel as she went about shaping the home where her

Son was going to grow. Instead, she had to plan. She had to make decisions—big ones and small ones. She had to get her hands dirty with the actual physical work of caring for a family, from carrying water to weaving clothes to teaching children. And she needed help too from her husband, Joseph; from her cousin Elizabeth; and no doubt from her family and Joseph's family back in Nazareth. She needed practical assistance and guidance for her ongoing choices.

The same thing is true of my young friend who started so far behind. Once she said yes to the Lord, she had a *lot* of work to do as well. She, too, needed help from her band of prayer partners, from her family, and especially from her Bible. And she, too, found the help she needed once she made the decision to say yes. She pursued a vision for what she was trying to do and started looking for help.

That last tactic—looking for help—is key. God truly does provide, but he also expects us to participate. He wants us actively involved in what he is doing in our lives. It's up to us to ask for help, to keep our eyes peeled for the Lord's provision, to accept with thanks, and then get on with the task of appropriating God's help into our lives.

God provides the scriptural guidance, for instance. But we have to actually read Scripture, figure out how it might be speaking to our lives, and then obey. He will provide friends and mentors. But we still may have to make the first move to actually get to know those people. He may provide us with a husband or close friends or family members to share the task of making a home and raising children. But we have to make important decisions about how we all get along—not to mention loving and helping our loved ones as well.

There's a reason the Father doesn't just hand us his gifts on a silver platter and provide our needs without participation on our part. That's because he wants more for us than just getting our needs met. He wants us to grow. He wants us to be part of his ongoing kingdom. He wants our bodies as well as our homes to be fit dwelling places for him. So even as he provides for us, he is also in the constant process of teaching us and refining us, shaping our homes and our lives to more closely reflect his wonderful reality.

Keeping all that in mind, what kinds of divine help are available for you as a mom, a keeper of holy ground…and what is your part in receiving them?

Most important, of course, is God's ongoing presence in the Holy Spirit. Jesus told us about that when he was nearing the end of his earthly ministry. Not only did he promise to prepare a place for us, he also promised to send us his constant presence in the form of the Holy Spirit, whose name actually translates as "Helper" (or Comforter, Counselor, Intercessor, Advocate, Strengthener, and Standby).

What an amazing thing to know—that the power of almighty God is available to help you in making the right choices for your home! Whenever you are feeling lonely or overwhelmed, whenever you are trying to decide whether to stay at home with your children or buy new furniture for the guest bedroom, or whenever you are (my personal favorite) biting your tongue to keep from saying the wrong thing or saying too much, you can always turn to the Holy Spirit for strength and comfort and guidance. Your part is to turn to the Lord in prayer, bring your dilemmas directly to him, and trust in his nearness. Even on those days when you cannot *feel* the Lord's presence—and believe me, there will be days like that—he will still be there, waiting for the moment when your spirit is still and your eyes are open. And when your faith begins to falter, you can always turn to the second resource God provides to all of us—his guidebook, the Bible.

I'm well aware that busy young women can be frustrated by being told to read their Bibles more. Bible study can sometimes feel like just one more task piled on to an overloaded schedule. But that's just the problem. We get into the habit of considering Bible reading an obligation—something we're doing for God—rather than a vital source of support—something God provides for us. I've learned over the years that that overloaded feeling is really just one more reason we need to be leaning *more* on God's living Word. Not because of guilt and obligation, but because we need the help.

How does the Bible help you with the task of shaping your home? To start with, it offers some extremely practical and specific instructions as to how you can live in your home as a woman of God—for instance, Proverbs 31; Galatians 3; Ephesians 5; and Titus 2. The Bible also contains a wealth of general guidance as to how to live as a godly human being—how to treat others, how to pray, how to understand what is most important in life. It offers comfort, encouragement, and motivation; it reminds us of God's love and providence, promises God's presence, and cautions about the consequences of choices for and against the Lord. In addition, it's full of great stories and inspiring role models—Naomi and Ruth, Hannah, Esther, Eunice and Lois, and, of course, Jesus' mother Mary—as well as some vivid examples of how *not* to live.

I truly believe there is no dilemma we can face in life for which Scripture does not provide a solution or point in the right direction. Granted, these answers are not always direct and specific— remember, God expects us to participate in our own help, and that means we sometimes have to dig deep. But I'm convinced that time spent in the Word will eventually yield the answers we seek, either through *prescription* (telling us directly what to do, as in Proverbs or some of Paul's letters), through *description* (providing an example or analogy in a story or event), or simply through the process of transforming our thinking until the answers seem clear. As busy as I know you are, I urge you to try to put aside some regular time both for studying the Bible in a disciplined way and for reading devotionally, simply letting the living Word minister to your heart, strengthening and supporting you as you live as part of the family of faith.

So we've looked at two dependable resources God provides to every one of his followers—his presence and his Word. The third resource he always supplies, in one way or another, is a family. And before you start protesting about the inadequacies of your particular combination of relatives, let me explain. While Jesus never ignored or denigrated his earthly biological family, he also made it clear that his real family is made up of those who follow him and do his Father's will. Once you have said the Big Yes to God, you are part of that family, the body of Christ. Your Father is God, your big brother is Jesus, and everyone in the world who has accepted Christ is your brother and sister.

More specifically, there is a branch of this beautiful family tree that is available to you as a source of support. I'm talking about a church, a formal or informal gathering of God's people. If you have said yes to God's calling for your home, you need to be part of a Bible-believing, faithful body of people in the area where you live. Involvement in a living, growing branch of Christ's family changed my life as a young, awkward girl from a very dysfunctional biological family. And while I have learned that church families can sometimes behave quite dysfunctionally as well, I have also seen God do amazing things through these gatherings of his people.

Never has this been so powerfully clear to me than in the months preceding our daughter's wedding, when our own church family rallied round us to help and support and celebrate. Of the 700 people who filled the sanctuary, only about a dozen were biologically linked to the bride and groom! The rest were our beloved family in Christ, and how grateful we were that God had gifted us with this caring congregation. They even built a special table to hold the wedding cake!

Psalm 68:6 says that the Lord "makes a home for the lonely." He also says, "Seek, and you will find" (Matthew 7:7). If you seek it, you will find a branch of the Lord's family that offers you support and involves you in its activities. Even more specifically, within Christ's family you will find your most important sources of help: mentors and sisters.

I have talked about this at length in other books (*Finding a Mentor, Being a Mentor* and *The Stay-at-Home Mom*), so I will only touch on this idea here. But essentially you need at least one older woman—older in experience as well as age—who can teach and guide you in what it means to shape a godly environment. This relationship is described in Titus 2:3-5, in which Paul recommends that older women teach younger women about how to live and how to run their homes. A mentor is someone who will listen to you, reassure you, and offer you wise advice. She is a role model, someone to look up to, a woman who is more experienced in both faith matters and home matters than you are, someone whose wisdom and accomplishments you can admire and emulate.

In addition to a mentor, however, you also need at least one person who is basically your peer, someone who can work alongside you and share your struggles. This is the kind of friend I call a sister—a buddy who will trade babysitting, meet you for coffee when you're feeling isolated, go with you to the paint store and give an opinion. She may be a casual acquaintance you see often and have a lot in common with or the lifelong friend who lives in another town but still manages to call you every week or so. A sister can be a true soul mate, or she can simply be a fellow traveler for a season of your life, but she should be someone who shares important values and life experience, someone whose company you enjoy, and someone who is willing to give and take in a helpful relationship.

A mentor and a sister—I am talking about the bare minimum here. In real life you might find a series of mentors for various aspects of your life: home care, parenting, marriage, home-based business, spiritual growth, caring for your aging parents, and whatever else is appropriate. You may have seasons when sisters abound and others when you long for a peer to share your life. In this area, in particular, it's important to remember that God knows what you need and will provide for you...but again, you are expected to participate.

Your part, to begin with, is to pray for the help you need. Ask the Lord to open your eyes to possible mentors and sisters. Trust him to send you the help you need. Then look around you—at church, in your neighborhood, at organizations you are part of. When you spot a possible mentor or sister, be prepared to make the first move.

To find a mentor, look for women whose wisdom and experience you can admire—not necessarily the obvious leaders, but women of solid background, whose lives clearly show evidence of spiritual fruit. When you spot someone like that, first spend time in prayer and then ask her if she would consider a mentoring relationship with you. Share with her the qualities in her life that you have noticed and tell her you would like those qualities in your life.

You may find that you need to do a little selling job on a potential mentor. She may not see herself as wise or experienced, or she may fear that mentoring will require too much of her. Reassure her that you don't expect her to be perfect and you don't want to monopolize her time. And don't push for a commitment right away; instead, ask her to pray about it.

It often helps to set parameters at the beginning—how often you will meet, where you will get together. It might even be a good idea to establish a future cut-off date for your times together—a time to reevaluate whether you will continue meeting together. A mentoring relationship might involve anything from sharing breakfast together once a month to a more intense one-on-one relationship. And even as you are looking for a mentor, keep in mind that you yourself are probably in a position to mentor a younger woman—sharing God's gift of support by passing along what you have learned.

How do you find a sister? It makes sense to look for her in your neighborhood, your Sunday school class, your local parent organization. But you may also run into her in the supermarket checkout line, in the office, or on the benches next to the playground. She is the woman whose laugh you are drawn to, whose comments you can relate to, who somehow attracts your interest. She may not be exactly like you—you may even seem quite different on the surface, but your belief systems are the same, and something in her spirit calls to yours.

OTTO'S MOTTO

You are who you hang out with.

When a woman like that comes to your notice, don't miss the opportunity. Ask her to share a cup of coffee. Suggest a playdate with your kids. Offer to help paint her basement or swap chores. Find a way to spend time together. And remember that sisterhood is a two-way proposition. A sister will be a source of help in your life, but you will need to help her too. A sister relationship is usually less formal than a mentoring relationship, but it needs to be a mutual one based on shared values. When God sends you a sister to support you, the best way you can participate in his provision is to give yourself to being a support in her life.

You've probably noticed that the process of finding mentors and sisters is basically a matter of establishing friendships. But these are special, deliberate friendships (intentionality, remember). You are consciously looking for friends who will help you grow and share your commitment to Christ. You are opening your life to God's provision of a family to support you as you continue to say yes to his call.

As long as we're talking about family, you might be wondering how your biological family fits into this scenario. To be perfectly honest, that depends on who you are. Your family of origin and your husband and children are certainly part of God's plan for your life, but how they fit into the support system for your home depends on who you are and who they are.

For some of you, your mother and father, brothers and sisters, and extended family are a beautiful source of love and support. Certainly, God intended this to be the case. Ideally, you learned at your mother's knee the skills you need to run a household smoothly, and she still serves you in a mentor fashion. Ideally, your father provided you with inspiration and leadership, and he also taught you what he knew about establishing a home and helping it function. Ideally, your siblings are brothers and sisters in Christ and your extended family provides you with love and support as well as prayer, genuinely helpful guidance, role models, and even practical help such as cribs, folding chairs, and friendly gatherings.

Ideally, too, your husband is a loving, supporting man who shares your vision for a home that honors God. Ideally, your children carry some of the workload of the household and have absorbed enough of your spiritual training to keep you reminded of what you are trying to do.

But the reality for so many of us is that our biological families just don't cut it when it comes to being supportive. Like me, you may have come from a critical, rejecting background, a place where people didn't keep their promises. Or perhaps your home was chaotic and disorganized. Your parents, siblings, and extended family may or may not be believers. So although even in this situation you may have received more help than you are aware of—I can see now that even my overly critical mother taught me a lot about how to get things done at home, and my Aunt Pat was my first beloved mentor—the truth is that you cannot always count on your biological family as a dependable source of support.

The same is true for your nuclear family, the people who actually share your home. Although the biblical ideal for a family consists of parents and children, husbands and wives, you may be living as a single mother. You may be married to an unbeliever or to a man who doesn't share your beliefs about what a home can be or simply to someone you feel is "the wrong man." You may be trying to care for your children and your parents at the same time. Your teenagers may bring you nothing but grief.

But even if these things are not true, if you're relying on your husband and children to be your support system—or even a big part of your support system—you may be in danger of putting too much pressure on those close relationships. Children, in particular, were never meant to be a support to their parents, at least not while they are minors. Yes, they should help with the work of being a family, but parents who lean on their children for emotional support do them a great disfavor.

And though your husband is meant to be your partner, your lover, and your leader, he is ill-equipped to be your sole source of support in running your household. Yes, you support each other mutually. But unless you rely on other sources—your Bible, the Holy Spirit, your mentors, and your sisters—you risk pulling your husband down instead of mutually supporting him. You *both* need love and support from the body of Christ to maintain your home as a place where God is honored and God's work is centered.

In addition to the three major sources of ongoing support God gives us—his presence, his Word, and his family—he provides other forms of support for specific times and specific purposes. There may be times in your life—there have been times in mine—when you may need advice or guidance from your pastor, a counseling professional, a teacher, a spiritual director, or some other human helper. There may be times when the most immediate or appropriate source of help and inspiration are books, magazines, radio, television, or videos. I myself have benefited profoundly from the wisdom of writers and speakers. And I certainly wouldn't spend my time writing books and preparing video curricula if I weren't convinced that these can offer help and support to other women! There may even be times when the specific, practical help of a maid service or a babysitter can be a true godsend. I truly believe that part of your responsibility as the shaper of your home is to take advantage of the help God makes available in whatever form it might take.

Should you seek out or start a support group? My answer would be yes and no. It is absolutely true that a group of like-minded women can be a wonderful source of help, encouragement, motivation, strength, and practical help—a whole roomful of sisters. The organization I started called Homemakers by Choice was founded with that purpose in mind. So is my group of chosen "Chaber" sisters, who pledged support to each other many years ago and have loved and prayed each other through a lifetime's worth of births, deaths, marriages, and everything in between, and my "Lilies" group of younger women, whom my friend Sandy and I have mentored for many years now. But in our culture, I fear a "support group" has come to mean "sympathy group," a place where people with similar problems go to air their frustrations.

And while that may have its place, that's really not the kind of support you need for shaping a godly home.

By support I don't just mean sympathy or finding someone who understands what you are going through. Instead, the kind of support I mean is a relationship that strengthens you in the Lord and encourages you to do what he wants you to do. I also mean practical, down-to-earth, hands-on help—the kind of help that prays for you, cleans your toilet when you're sick, or takes your kids for a weekend so you can go on a silent retreat.

That kind of help can come from anyone who loves you in the Lord and is obedient to his guidance, not just someone who shares your particular problems. That's the kind of support to pray for—confident that the Lord who shaped your heart and wants your home to reflect his beauty will provide what you need to make it happen.

A Moment of
REFLECTION

1. What kinds of help do you feel most in need of right now in your life? Where does most of the support you feel come from?

2. What barriers—emotional, scheduling, financial—stand in the way of your taking advantage of the help God provides?

A Biblical Role Model

An excellent wife, who can find? For her worth is far above jewels.

The heart of her husband trusts in her, and he will have no lack of gain.

She does him good and not evil all the days of her life.

She looks for wool and flax and works with her hands in delight.

She is like merchant ships; she brings her food from afar.

She rises also while it is still night and gives food to her household and portions to her maidens.

She considers a field and buys it; from her earnings she plants a vineyard.

She girds herself with strength and makes her arms strong.

She senses that her gain is good; her lamp does not go out at night.

She stretches out her hands to the distaff, and her hands grasp the spindle.

She extends her hand to the poor, and she stretches out her hands to the needy.

She is not afraid of the snow for her household, for all her household are clothed with scarlet.

She makes coverings for herself; her clothing is fine linen and purple.

Her husband is known in the gates, when he sits among the elders of the land.

She makes linen garments and sells them, and supplies belts to the tradesmen.

Strength and dignity are her clothing, and she smiles at the future.

She opens her mouth in wisdom, and the teaching of kindness is on her tongue.

She looks well to the ways of her household, and does not eat the bread of idleness.

Her children rise up and bless her; her husband also, and he praises her, saying:

"Many daughters have done nobly, but you excel them all."

Charm is deceitful and beauty is vain, but a woman who fears the LORD, she shall be praised.

Give her the product of her hands, and let her works praise her in the gates.

PROVERBS 31:10-31

— SEVEN —

A YOU FOR
ALL SEASONS

Your home is holy ground. You are holy ground.

But, as important as your home is, you are *not* your home.

As important as your roles as wife, mother, homemaker, bread-winner, or hostess are, you are not defined by the roles you fill. You are, first of all, God's child. He knows you by name and by heart, and he never limits you to the labels we humans like to apply.

He made you as a woman, but to him you are never "just a woman."

He may have given you a husband—or allowed you to choose one—but to him you'll always be more than "just a wife."

He may have blessed you with children, but to him you are far more important than your capacity as a mother.

To the Lord, you are first and foremost you. You are his beloved. He wants you to grow, be responsible, abide in him, and be obedient. He wants you to reach out to others and work with him in bringing about his kingdom—in your home and outside of it. But his plans for you will never be limited to the place where you now find yourself. Whether you are single, married, widowed, or divorced; whether you are well-heeled or struggling; whether your kids are toddlers, tweens, teens, or even adults—you can be sure of two things:

First, you are called to be faithful and content in your present role.

Second, God has something wonderful in store for you, and he wants you to live in joyful anticipation of that future.

It's human nature to chafe a little at where we are, to want to move on or yearn for what we've left behind. It's also human nature to become so caught up in the hurly-burly of now that we *forget* there's more. If you're not yet a mother, you may long to get your family started. If you're a mother with a household of rambunctious children, you may long for your childless days. If you're up to your neck in errands, you may wish you had the freedom to contemplate and write. If your nest is empty, you may long for something to enliven your quiet house.

OTTO'S MOTTO

Your home is holy ground.
And you are holy ground!

That's where the twin principles of faithfulness and contentment, combined with joyful anticipation, can help you a lot. It's helped me a lot in my own life.

No matter where you are, you can be confident that God put you there. You can find something to learn, even if it's simply patience and endurance. You can probably find something to enjoy and be grateful for, even if it's a moment of quiet in the bathroom or a latte with friends at Starbucks. You can seek for guidance, pray for strength, embrace your family, and do what you can to make your home as close to heaven as possible.

In the meantime, though, I hope you'll be stuffing your files for the future.

I'm talking about both literal files and mental ones.

Mental files are your dreams for what you might want to be when your children grow up...or when *you* grow up. They're whispers from the Holy Spirit about what God has in store for the next chapter in your life. They are mental pictures of the next stage—

the last child in kindergarten, going back to school, finding a new career—and what you might be called to do. They might even be mental images of what your home will be like once you've removed the outlet plugs and baby locks on the cabinets!

No matter what your season in life, I urge you to keep those mental files open. Try to think about the future—I assure you that God is doing just that where you're concerned. Keep your dreams and hopes alive, but also try to keep an open mind for what God wants to teach you.

And whenever possible, I urge you to put the contents of your mental files on paper. Write them down in journal form. Shape them into desires and goals. (There's a difference. Desires are what you'd like to see. Goals are what you can actually, by yourself, achieve.) Store them in actual files in an actual file cabinet...or a cardboard box...or a computer file somewhere where you can find them and refer to them from time to time.

There's no limit to what you can store in your actual files for the future. A "how-to" article on a skill you'd like to develop. A newspaper story that touches your heart and calls to something deep within. (God may be calling you to minister someday in that area.) A list of things you want to accomplish before you die. A profile of someone in a career you'd like to try. The results of a temperament test you have taken to understand yourself and your personality better. (If you're interested in taking such a test, I personally recommend the one you'll find in a book called *Please Understand Me: Character and Temperament Types* by David Kiersey and Marilyn Bates, published in 1984 by Prometheus Nemesis.)

How deliberate and organized you are about this kind of file stuffing will depend on a lot of factors—your personality, your circumstances, and your level of contentment or discontentment. But the process of thinking ahead to the next season and the season after that can actually help you be more content and productive now and make wiser decisions about how you spend your time. It can also help you be ready for the next phase of your life when it arrives—even with such mundane matters as insurance and home remodeling. (David and I planned the guesthouse on our property, for instance, in anticipation of a day when we may need to downsize and be cared for by someone who loves us.)

But the most important benefit I've found in stuffing my files for the future is that it helps me remember that God sees beyond my current roles to the person I am and the person I am becoming. God loved me and blessed me when I was a young, gawky girl in a desperately unhappy home, when I was a young real estate agent, when I was newly married and moving every few years, when my daughter was small and as she grew, when I began speaking more and writing books. Now, when my husband is newly retired, my daughter is newly married, and my career seems to be gaining momentum, God loves me and blesses me still, and he wants to work through me to change the world.

And that really is where it starts…and where it will end.

Your home is holy ground, and so are you. You are blessed among women, and God has a plan for you and for your home. I hope you'll start there and carry it as far as you can. I hope you'll be able to say, whatever your role and whatever the season of your life, "As for me and my house, we will serve the LORD" (Joshua 24:15).

A Moment of REFLECTION

1. Purchase two brightly colored file folders. On one tab, write "Present Contentment" and on the other write "Future Hope" (or something like that). (Note: Instead of a file folder, you can also begin two small journals or scrapbooks. But I like files because they don't require any extra cutting or pasting.)

2. Make a list of five things about your current life for which you are thankful. Offer your list to God in prayer and then drop your list in the "Present Contentment" folder. Make a note to add something else to the folder within the next week.

3. Make another list of ten to a hundred things you've always wanted to do but never had a chance to try, or things you'd like to do before you die. Offer these items to God in prayer and drop your list into your "Future Hope" folder. Make a decision to add something else to this folder within the next week. (Doing this will probably help you start stuffing those mental file folders.)

Citizens of Heaven

*W*e are not citizens of this world trying to make our way to heaven; we are citizens of heaven trying to make our way through this world...we live as those who are on a journey home; a home we know will have the lights on, and the door open, and our Father waiting for us when we arrive. That means in all adversity our worship of God is joyful, our life is hopeful, our future is secure. There is nothing we can lose on earth that can rob us of the treasures God has given us and will give us.

THE LANDISFARNE,
via *The Anglican Digest*

PART TWO

Making Your Home a Place of Love and Peace

꩜

*Rejoice, be made complete, be comforted, be like-minded,
live in peace; and the God of love and peace will be with you.*

2 Corinthians 13:11

EIGHT

PEACE ON PURPOSE

I'VE ALWAYS HEARD THAT HOME is supposed to be a peaceful place," the young woman told me. "But to be honest, my home is just another source of stress. In fact, it's my main source of stress. Being at home just means more pressure, more irritations, more work to be done. The kids are always squabbling and talking back. My husband and I argue a lot. The house is a wreck. I seem to pick up constantly, but things don't seem to get better. I can't go anywhere in my home without having some undone chore staring me in the face.

"Don't get me wrong," she sighed. "I love my family. But sometimes I just want to run away from home. Anything for a little peace and quiet."

The sad truth is, the average home in average America these days is not a peaceful place for anyone—wives, husbands, mothers, children, singles. It's far from the refuge it was meant to be.

Instead, too typically, home is a chore pit, the place that shames us with the guilt of what we should be doing but don't have time for. It can be a sparring ring where we take out our frustrations on those we love best. For many, home is the place we hurry to leave in the morning, and then rush to take care of when we get home. A home contains beds where we pitch ourselves headlong after an exhausting day, only to pull ourselves out exhausted in the morning.

In the midst of it all, don't you long for peace? Don't you long for the serenity of a comfortable home, of a family that enjoys being together, a place that is removed from the rat race and yet lively and productive as well? Everybody needs a refuge, after all. The world is stressful, and it's hard to overestimate the value of a place that opens its arms and soothes our spirits. But we shouldn't have to run away from home to find that kind of place. Wouldn't it be better to make our homes into a place of love, refuge, and peace, a place that nurtures the spirit of everyone who lives there or visits?

I'm here to tell you that you can grow that kind of peace in your house. Your home, be it ranch style or city apartment or Winnebago, can be a refuge of peace, an antidote to a stressed-out, hurried culture, a space where the peace of God permeates and where all of you—even mom—find rest and strength.

But it won't happen by accident.

I have recently become aware that the idea of peace and harmony in the home is a very basic and important principle in the Jewish faith. It's called *shalom bayit,* and it has implications for everything from the relationship of husband and wife to the rules of a synagogue to a teenaged quarrel in the home. This Talmudic principle is mostly about relational peace, but it is related to all areas of family life. When a Jewish mother lights the candles at dinner to signify the beginning of the Sabbath, for example, she is also affirming the sense that her home is a peaceful refuge from the outside world and the Sabbath itself is a refuge from the stresses of the workaday week. Interpreters of this tradition have even held that certain lies can be justified in the interest of keeping peace at home.

Well, I don't know about the lies. But I do believe that we can learn something important from this concept of *shalom bayit.* It can teach us about intentional peace, about deliberately setting our homes apart and working to make them calm havens in an often stressful and chaotic world.

The truth is, if you want your home to be a peaceful place that you and your family long to come home to, you have to do it on purpose. You need to spend time considering the kind of atmosphere you want and the choices that will make a peaceful home a reality.

If you consult a decorating magazine, the choices you'll read about will almost certainly have something to do with paint and candles. You'll read words like "atmosphere" and "ambience" and, depending on what is popular at the moment, you'll be instructed to invest in "cozy clutter" or "clean simplicity" or "calming earth tones." (I've been around long enough to realize that the specifics change.)

I absolutely believe that the way you decorate and arrange your home can help make it a haven of peace. In fact, one of my favorite things to do is to redecorate and redesign my home to make it more welcoming and more useful and to serve our purposes better. Changes in the physical environment really can affect us emotionally and even spiritually.

But decorating is still only surface dressing. If you truly want your home to be a haven of rest in a hectic world, you need to dig deeper. You need to give some thought to what is making your home stressful. Then you need to start making the changes that will turn your stressful chore pit into the peaceful haven God intended it to be.

Where to start? Remember the picture on the front of the puzzle box? The place to start is envisioning what a peaceful home is like and noticing what may be disturbing the peace in your current home environment. When you do that, you can start to realize steps you can take to create a peaceful refuge for those around you.

So...what does a peaceful home look and feel like? It's easy to pinpoint what it's *not* like. Words like "stress" and "pressure" come to mind. So do bad attitudes: complaining, whining, nagging, bickering, selfishness, rebellion, and disobedience. Frustration and irritation, sensory discomfort, unresolved arguments from the past or noisy present ones. A dirty, cluttered house rarely feels like a peaceful refuge (though it might feel like a place to hide from the world). Neither does a noisy, conflict-filled one.

Silence is certainly no guarantee of peace—though a peaceful home makes room for silence. A house that vibrates with unspoken resentment or echoes with loneliness and futility is not a refuge. A house where nobody dares rock the boat or ask questions is not peaceful. And a house can be lively or even noisy and still have that sense of underlying, abiding peace. It can be full of purposeful activity and still be quiet. It can ring with laughter and still resonate with calm.

When I talk about peace and quiet, I'm not talking about an absence of activity or sound, but a spiritual presence—an atmosphere that communicates, in the words of medieval mystic Julian of Norwich, that "all will be well, all shall be well, and all manner of things will be well."

I think of a peaceful home as a place that is *emotionally* peaceful—safe, consistent, cheerful, encouraging, motivating, and energizing, filled with a sense of the sacred, not frantic or stressful. Often there is a sense of celebration or even joy, and fun is seldom absent. Even if you live alone, it should be a place that fosters your peace of mind.

I think, too, of a home that is *relationally* peaceful—where conflicts are faced wisely (not ignored or hidden), where both authority and autonomy is respected, where everyone feels a strong sense of "we" and pulls together to help the place run smoothly.

Whatever the décor, a true refuge is *physically* peaceful. Think of a home that is ordered and organized, comfortable and comforting, well maintained and reasonably clean. A peaceful home bears the marks of purposeful effort, but it invites you to rest as well as work.

In this particular day and age, a *chronologically* peaceful home is a true refuge. This means a home where schedules are under control, where life is purposeful and planned, and space is made for rest. "Hurry up" is a rare admonishment, and the panic of searching for shoes or car keys at the last moment is only a memory. The chaos and panic of time pressure is replaced by a sense that there really is time for whatever is truly important.

A truly peaceful home is *spiritually* peaceful. It is modeled on God's plan for the home, including God-ordained roles and patterns of authority. Yes means yes. No means no. Respectful and appropriate conversation replaces bickering and back talk. Prayer shapes the atmosphere. Love fills the air. The peace you feel is God's peace.

At this point I hope you're feeling inspired instead of overwhelmed or defeated—because this kind of peace is within your reach. In fact, I believe you are being called to be a peacemaker in your home. You have the opportunity and the responsibility to create a sacred and peaceful space in your four walls, a place where the Prince of Peace reigns.

A true haven of calm in a frantic, chaotic world.

It's another task that's really worth saying yes to.

A Moment of
REFLECTION

1. What is the most peaceful place you've ever visited? What do you think contributed to that atmosphere of peace?

2. Did you grow up in a peaceful home? How do you think your upbringing contributes to the way you live in your own home?

3. Do you have any conflicts when you think of making your home peaceful? Does peaceful sound like "boring" to you? Does it sound like "keeping the peace at all costs," including not being honest with those you live with?

4. What elements in your own home make it feel less than peaceful?

---❦❧---

CREATING A
PEACEFUL AMBIENCE

True peace in a home is based on peaceful hearts and peaceful relationships, but a little attention to the physical aspects of the home can help a home feel like a peaceful refuge.

- ❧ Keep it clean. *It's hard to feel peaceful in an environment that is grubby, sticky, or unsanitary.*

- ❧ Keep it clear. *Clutter can be visually stressful. Try to keep surfaces relatively clear, even if it means (temporarily), piling all the extra stuff in a box and hiding it away. Resist using flat surfaces for storage.*

- ❧ Keep it cozy. *"Clean and uncluttered" doesn't have to mean sterile or antiseptic. Soft pillows, cozy throws, comfortable seating, and soft lighting all contribute to a sense of safety and security.*

- ❧ Use sound to create a sense of peace. *Quiet music is a time-tested way to "soothe the savage beast."*

- ❧ Use good scents. *Pleasant aromas can do a lot toward making your house feel like a peaceful refuge. Try a drop of aromatic oil on a light bulb ring, a fragrant bouquet, a spritz of perfume in closet, or a loaf of bread in the oven.*

NINE

THE CLICK OF
THE THERMOSTAT

I AM A HOT-NATURED WOMAN WHO HAS LIVED nearly half of her life in the very, very hot state of Arizona. This means I have developed a very intimate relationship with both thermostats and thermometers.

When the mercury starts creeping up, and Phoenix settles in for one of our hundred-plus months, I love to hear the little click that tells me the air conditioning is doing its job and I can spend my day being active and efficient instead of languishing in the heat.

So I know well the difference between a thermostat and a thermometer. The thermometer just tells me what I already know—that the temperature is rising and if nothing is done I'll soon be able to barbecue on the back patio without a grill. But a thermostat actually *does* something about the temperature. When it registers a rising temperature, it clicks into action. It does whatever is necessary to make the air cool and comfortable again. (Back in Chicago, where I grew up, the thermostat was just as important to keep houses warm and cozy.)

What does this have to do with making your home a haven of rest? Well, you've heard the saying "If Mama ain't happy, ain't nobody happy." More than most of us would like to admit, that's true. Women tend to be the mood setters for the home. Perhaps it's because we tend to be more home oriented or because we are more involved in the day-to-day activities of the house. Perhaps it's because we're often more sensitive to minute changes of atmosphere. Whatever the reason, our attitudes and our efforts have influence. And if we make peacefulness a priority in our lives, our very house will "catch" it.

How do you set the emotional and spiritual thermostat in your home to "peace"? Obviously, by what you do and say, but even more profoundly by who you are inside. If you sing while you wash dishes or mope when you don't get your way, those actions will influence the atmosphere. If you are distant and distracted, the "temperature" is likely to dip. If you are anxious and depressed, the household will feel tense and cold. If you are warm and exuberant, your household will respond accordingly.

One of the best ways to make your home a haven of God's peace, therefore, is to cultivate that peace in your own heart. The more you nurture a vision of peace, the more you make peace a priority, the more you work to create an orderly and upbeat environment, the more deeply that peace will root itself in your family life.

Domestic peacemaking, in other words, works best from the inside out. It starts with welcoming God's peace into your own heart and letting that peace touch every aspect of your daily life. The advice the apostle Paul gave to the Philippians gives us a picture of how this can work in our homes as well:

> Rejoice in the Lord always; again I will say, rejoice!…Be anxious for nothing, but in everything by prayer and supplication with thanksgiving let your requests be made known to God. And the peace of God, which surpasses all comprehension, will guard your hearts and your minds in Christ Jesus. Finally, brethren, whatever is true, whatever is honorable, whatever is right, whatever is pure, whatever is lovely, whatever is of good repute, if there is any excellence and if anything worthy of praise, dwell on these

things. The things you have learned and received and
heard and seen in me, practice these things, and the God
of peace will be with you (Philippians 4:4-9).

How do you cultivate a peaceful heart? You draw near to the
Lord and rejoice that he is near to you. You rest in the knowledge
that he cares for you. You pray about everything. You "dwell" on
what is right and good.

Shall I be more specific? You cultivate a peaceful heart by
spending regular time with the Prince of Peace. You study God's
Word and read it devotionally to become better acquainted with
him. You look for quiet places and set aside quiet time (a challenge
in itself) where you can stop, sit, and stay on a regular basis,
soaking in his presence. You speak to God, and then you listen,
meditating on his goodness and practicing doing right until his
peace literally becomes welded into your being.

I know that all this may feel like just another set of chores you
need to accomplish in an already packed schedule. Especially if
you have young children at home, you may be hard pressed to find
a quiet second. Or when you do manage to find a quiet second,
you may honestly prefer to spend it reading a novel or taking a
long bath rather than sitting before the Lord.

But the simple truth is that unless you make the time to get
quiet before the Lord, you won't be able to live quietly or peacefully—because God is the ultimate source of peace at home and
elsewhere. And if you aren't living within God's peace, you'll find it
hard to switch your home's emotional thermostat in a peaceful
direction.

It's important to remember that whatever fills your heart and
your mind is going to spill out in your words and actions and attitudes. You won't be able to fake peace if you are anxious and your
spirit is tied up in knots. You won't be able to set the thermostat to
quiet confidence if you're seething with anger and resentment and
frustration. So, if you are serious about setting the thermostat
toward peace in your home and making it a haven of love for

everyone who lives there, you need to do what you can to set *your* thermostat, and the only way to do that is through regular time with the Lord.

An old woman once told me that when she was growing up, no one was hungry or thirsty until her mama finished praying. In other words, everyone in the house knew that mama's quiet time came first; snacks and drinks of water simply had to wait. Don't underestimate the peace that fills a home that operates on this basis. It's a peace that comes from learning to lean on the Lord, to trust him and his authority, to put him first, to cultivate a peaceful heart.

A peaceful heart comes from trust in God and confidence in who you are—his beloved child. That kind of calm confidence was a hallmark of Jesus' ministry.

Remember the story from the Gospels where Jesus slept in a boat in the middle of a storm? (Mark 4:35-41). Now that's a picture of a peaceful heart—to be able to lie down and slumber away while the waves are slamming into you and threatening to sink your boat. The disciples were frantic, but Jesus remained absolutely calm, confident in his conviction that God was in charge and would take care of him. He was also confident in the authority the Father had given him, the ability to calm the waves and bring peace wherever he found himself.

OTTO'S MOTTO

A goal is not the same as a desire.

That kind of confidence can be ours as well, but it is sometimes hard-won. Though God's love and salvation are free gifts, learning to trust in his care can be a struggle. It certainly won't happen overnight. Cultivating a peaceful heart takes practice and perseverance; it needs to be a goal and a subject of prayer. In your quiet times of reading God's Word, praying and listening, and just being in the presence of your Father, you gradually come to understand what God's peace is all about.

A peaceful heart also comes from a clear understanding of what you are trying to do, why you are doing it, and who makes it possible in the first place. So it makes sense to spend some of your time apart focusing on the purpose of your life, the principles that drive you, and the priorities that guide your decisions. Once you have clarified these issues for yourself, you'll take a much more serene approach to daily challenges—and you'll be much more effective in your efforts to wield the authority he has given you to make your home a haven of peace.

Purpose, principles, and priorities—they all sound a bit alike, and they're all somewhat related. So it might be helpful at this point to clarify what exactly I mean when I speak of these "three Ps."

Basically, a *purpose* is a reason and a motivation—it's a belief about why we are in a certain circumstance and what we want to do while we are there. A purpose can be specific—that's what finding your purpose as a mom is all about. But even more important than your purpose as a mom—or wife, teacher, athlete, or whatever your specific calling—is your larger purpose as a human being.

Why do you believe you're in this world? What do you want to accomplish in the course of your lifetime, and what do you believe God wants you to accomplish? You would be surprised at how considering these questions helps you focus your mind, simplify your efforts, and live much more peacefully.

I often urge the women I work with to take some time and much prayer and then actually write down a brief (maybe ten-word) "life phrase" or statement of purpose that reflects their understanding of why they are on earth and what they want to accomplish. My own life phrase, which I review every year is now 30 years old: "To share the joy of my life with others through my enthusiasm, example, teaching, actions, and perseverance." In recent years I have added another phrase: "To enhance daily the truth of God to the next generation." This summary of why I believe I'm here and what I've been called to do has been the basis for all the other goals I have pursued since then. And you'd be amazed at how it's worked to clarify my thinking, help make difficult decisions, and renew my confidence that my life matters to God. It helps me live up to the words of Isaiah: "The steadfast of mind You will keep in perfect peace, because he trusts in You" (Isaiah 26:3). By building my confidence and helping me hold steady, my statement of purpose helps quiet my heart.

Principles, too, have been important tools to help me set my personal and domestic thermostat to peace. A principle is a guide for behavior that holds true in any situation. It's not a rigid rule, but it's not a mere suggestion either. Rather, it's a watchword, a statement of what is right, a personal guideline that influences all my decisions. The Ten Commandments are essentially a list of principles. So are many of the Proverbs. The Epistle writers in the New Testament set down principles that are still changing lives today.

The top five principles I have chosen to drive my own life are: (1) being a woman of my word, (2) being honest, (3) being neat, (4) respecting and listening to others, and (5) being a hard worker. I believe that if I manage to live by these principles, I'll come close to being the woman God has in mind for me to be.

How does living by principle help me cultivate a quiet heart and establish a peaceful home? Mostly by reinforcing right behavior and removing options. They keep me from having to reinvent the wheel every day.

If I'm determined to live by the principle of being a hard worker, for instance, I automatically rule out certain choices. I don't have the option of watching hours of TV every day. I don't have the option of giving up on an unpleasant chore. I don't have to agonize whether to sweep the porch or scrub the tub. I just do it, hopefully with a cheerful attitude.

It's interesting to note that in the Bible, peace and righteousness are inseparably intertwined. Psalm 72:7 puts it this way: "In his days may the righteous flourish, and abundance of peace till the moon is no more." And Psalm 85:10 says, "Righteousness and peace have kissed each other." Because living by principle helps me live righteously, it only makes sense that it promotes peace in my heart as well.

I can't overemphasize the importance of living by principle. Principles are what enable us to stick to a right path and resist the pressures of the outside culture and our own sinful desires. I've often told women that unless they believe in a principle, they shouldn't even attempt to pick up a practical hint based on that principle and do it. Without that undergirding belief in a principle, the good habit will be gone in one to six weeks.

One silly but helpful way I've found to remind myself of important principles in my life and communicate them to others is the use of catchwords and sayings. We've done this in our house since my daughter was little, and our "Otto's Mottos" have turned out to be not only helpful teaching tools, but also builders of family unity. Our mottos remind us that a peaceful home is a principled home, one driven by convictions, not circumstances.

See—there's a motto right there: Live by conviction, not circumstances! It's concise, it's memorable, it helps me remember to live from the inside out and not be overwhelmed by the outside world. My mottoes have helped me so much that I've included them throughout this book in the hope they'll stick in your mind and help you in the task of creating and maintaining a holy home.

Establishing and sticking to your *priorities* is yet another way to cultivate a peaceful heart by simplifying your decisions. Priorities are quite simply what matters most to you, what you will choose first if circumstances demand that you must choose among the loyalties in your life.

The sad truth, especially to enthusiastic "doers" like me, is that none of us can do everything. There simply aren't enough hours in a day—and I know I don't have the energy. I also know that cramming too much into my schedule is a surefire way to rob me and my household of the peace we crave. So how do I choose between attractive activities and worthwhile commitments? By keeping a firm grasp on my priorities.

OTTO'S MOTTO

Live by conviction, not circumstances.

But how do I determine my priorities? I know that my priorities should be God, my family, and myself, but those very general categories can be less than helpful. If I said yes to every opportunity to serve God at church and through speaking and writing, I would never even see my family, and that cannot be what the Lord wants. Years ago, I learned a more helpful way of approaching priorities, which is to ask myself about any possible involvement: "Can someone else do it?"

Asking that question is a quick and accurate way to determine what my priorities have to be. Only the activities for which I answer no truly qualify as a priority.

Note that I don't ask, "Can someone else do this as well as me?" That question is a trap for anyone who tends to think her way of doing things is the right way. I almost never think that someone else's way is better than mine. But when I ask myself, "Can someone else do it?" I quickly realize that only a few of my life commitments really qualify. In fact, I've narrowed mine down to five:

- *Nurturing my relationship with God.* No one else can pray my prayers, study the Bible for me, or nurture a close friendship with the Prince of Peace.

- *Taking care of myself as a person and growing to be the person God wants me to be.* Nobody else can exercise my body or feed my mind.

- *Being David Otto's wife.* Other people can know him or even love him, but no one else can care for him and support him as his wife.

- *Being Anissa Otto's mother.* She will never have another!

- *Managing my household.* Even if I have help, I'm still the one with the ultimate responsibility.

This doesn't mean I never commit to an activity that's not part of my basic priorities. I often do. I teach. I speak. I write books. I go out with my girlfriends and have fun. All those things are activities that matter to me. But if I'm not taking care of fundamental priorities, I must rethink my other involvements.

Do you see how establishing priorities can help you maintain a calm spirit and a quiet heart by keeping you from being stretched too thin? Like the principles that guide your life, your priorities make your decisions easier. They cut down on feelings of guilt over having to say no. They boost your confidence and lift your spirits... not to mention setting your thermostat to peace.

A Moment of
REFLECTION

1. What kinds of activities help you keep a peaceful heart?

2. Take several days to formulate your own "life phrase" or statement of overall purpose. Write it down in a notebook or journal and then go back and review it over a period of time. Does it still hold true? Does it still help you make decisions? How does your life phrase help you set the thermostat for your home?

3. Can you list five basic principles that guide your life—not that *should* drive your life, but that actually do? What does listing these principles show you about your motivations and your daily activities?

4. Based on the explanation in this chapter, what do your priorities need to be? What items in your life can only *you* do?

Who Holds the Heart of This Home?

There is a wonderful place,
a space so secure and warm,
that all who are privileged to live there
call it home.

Who holds the heart of this home?

The walls are colored with laughter
and the floors with wall-to-wall memories.
Each space testifies to the
bustling energy and joy of blended lives.

Who holds the heart of this home?

It's more than an address
or a statement of achievement and style.
It's a tender oasis from the storms of daily life,
a place of peace and rest.

Who holds the heart of this home?

Cheerleaders for life dwell here
as do living testimonies for faith.
Imperfect saints work out the walk of wisdom
in the halls of this home.

Who holds the heart of this home?

For every damaged day and sharp defeat,
home is the balm for the wound.
For every cutting word and ungracious event,
home is the kindness we crave.

Who holds the heart of this home?

And every bad memory of family and childhood
is swallowed in the embrace of a now happy home.
The time for forgiveness and healing is here
in the sanctuary of home.

Who holds the heart of this home?

So, those who build a home instead of a house,
a deliberate and prayer-laced place
rather than a sterile designer's delight,
do well.

Who holds the heart of this home?

You hold the heart of this home.

David and Donna Otto

TEN

A COUNTERCULTURAL
CALM

JESUS SAID IT TO HIS DISCIPLES during his last night on earth: "Peace I leave with you; My peace I give to you; not as the world gives do I give to you" (John 14:27).

If you take a minute to think, you'll realize that the peace "the world gives" is not very peaceful at all. That's exactly Jesus' point. The world has never been a particularly peaceful place, and what peace it offers is not very dependable. Today, it seems, unpeaceful chaos rushes by at a heightened pace. When it comes to our use of time, especially, our current culture seems to be out of control—and all too often we and our families are caught up in the crunch.

When I speak around the country, I often tell women that our culture has changed the "shape" of time. By that I mean the way our culture looks at and uses time has changed in the past 60 years or so.

If you are old enough, you may remember that time used to come in the form of slow-moving, lazy afternoons with no discernable beginning and very little end except the call to supper. The TV was silent or nonexistent. Books and quiet playtimes were filled with creative imaginings about anything and everything. And the clock ran slow—sometimes painfully slow if you were waiting for a special event or visit.

This is the shape of time as our grandmothers and even mothers knew it. Time flowed, and we flowed with it. People worked, of course, but the emphasis was on the doing, not getting it done and moving immediately to something else. Daily and weekly and seasonal routines were dependable but rarely frantic. Time consisted of indefinite sequential chunks of "now." We spent time connected to our surrounding natural world and with the people God brought into our life.

Much of the less developed world still lives with this slower approach to time. Phrases like "Latin time" or "African time" are shorthand ways of saying that time in these other cultures is flexible and schedules are approximations, not deadlines. Americans who travel to such places often find themselves frustrated with such a slow and relational pace of life; and visitors from less "developed" countries often feel confused and ill at ease over how fast most Americans do things.

Instead of a regular and seamless flow, time has been made a measured commodity. We slice and dice time into discrete units, each smaller and smaller, and we measure success by how much we can accomplish in a set amount of time. For most of us, busyness has become a source of pride, a measure of our worth. Unfortunately, many of us are paying the price for this busyness in the form of stress and pressure in our hearts and in our homes. Instead of a rest and a refuge, home becomes just another part of the pressure cooker.

What caused this radical shift in the world's view of time? Technology undoubtedly has played a big role. Almost all of us, willingly or unwillingly, are now connected to the technological revolution—and it's a 24-hours-a-day, seven-days-a-week proposition. Because technology enables us to cram more and more into our days, we've become accustomed to doing just that. We've become so accustomed to being always "on call" that we've almost forgotten what real downtime is like.

A related contributor to our cultural time crunch is the deluge of information that pours down on all of us every day. It is said that an educated man in seventeenth-century Europe could know everything then known to Western culture. Today, the total quantity of available information doubles every 18 months. No one can know all or even a substantial portion of it. And while a lot of the information in newspapers, magazines, TV, radio, newsletters, and the Internet is useful, much of it is not. The average person is exposed to more than 3000 advertising messages a day through spam e-mails, telemarketer calls during dinner, inserts in our mail, TV and radio commercials, and even rented movies.

The very fact that we are exposed to all this increased information means we must deal with it on one level or another. Even the decision to ignore a message takes time and energy. Where an actual informed decision is needed, we can get quick access to a lot of relevant data, but often that data just increases the number of available choices.

And that's yet another aspect of the time crunch in today's society: the almost infinite array of options we face in almost every situation. In rural America a few decades back, it was common to have only one choice in telephones: a black wall phone connected to a party line. Today we should blush in embarrassment at the number and nature of the options for phones. And not just styles and types of phones or even phone rate packages, but phone numbers as well!

The very fact that so many choices are required from us depletes the time available for us to do other things. It also means that we learn to make lots of choices quickly, and life speeds up. My friend Barry, observing this increased pace of life, says that his mother walked through life, that he is jogging through life, and that his daughter is running! I wonder how he will describe the pace of life for his granddaughter, should he be so blessed as to have one. Flying, maybe?

OTTO'S MOTTO

There's always time to do
what God asks us to do.

Yet another time eater in our culture seems to be a direct result of our technology-driven, high-information, multiple-choice society. Increasingly, our time is devoured and our irritation levels are raised by inefficient, customer-unfriendly, and sometimes deceptive bureaucratic structures. Computer snafus, impersonal service, and "stealth" charges on our credit cards are annoyingly common. And because we live at high speed, we often don't even question or protest. We just maneuver our way through the phone menus, wait for the clerk to figure out the change, let the extra charge slide by, all the while feeling abused, until our rising irritation levels reach blow-up levels. Unfortunately, we're likely to blow up at a family member or an innocent employee, and nothing is done to change the system.

Affluence has also influenced our changed view of time. By world standards we are a wealthy nation, and this affluence shows up in the way we live. The average new house today is almost twice as large as the average new home built 30 years ago. We live farther from our places of work and drive to get there, which means we often have more than one car. Our commute extends the workday and eats up time that would otherwise be devoted to home tasks or leisure. And we are working long hours simply to support our busy and acquisitive lifestyles.

What do we do with the money we make in our long workweeks? According to statistics, we are more likely to spend it than save it. Our very economy, we are told, depends on our spending. The level of consumer confidence is carefully measured each quarter and influences the stock market and economic planning throughout the country.

What kind of things do we buy? Just look around your house. Chances are, it is filled with lots of nice-to-have but nonessential items. Many show up in multiples—cars, computers, toaster ovens, not to mention shoes. The trouble is, all those things we buy—even "time saving" items—often end up taking our time from us. Appliances have to be maintained. Technology and toys break down and need fixing. Clothes require cleaning. A Lou

Hams poll found the leisure time of the average American family declined 37 percent between 1973 and 1999. As Karl E. Johnson said, "The cycle of consumption leaves us rich in things but poor in time."

Despite the shift in the shape of time, most of us women are still responsible for home and family. Many have added the role of breadwinner to our duties. We also give ourselves away to volunteer services and church activities and keep up relational connections with extended family and friends. We earnestly try to spend time with the Lord through prayer, Bible study, and church. We still strive to do it all. But in order to do it all, we have to function in fast-forward speed—which means that life becomes a series of tasks.

Each task seems necessary to keep the train of life running for our family and ourselves. So we use a planner to help us get organized. We use some of our affluence to buy servants to help us with the tasks—usually the kind of electronic servants that plug into the wall. And, of course, we multitask routinely.

If you have a man in your life, you may have noticed that he is not as geared toward multitasking as you are. Not long ago David came to me and proudly announced that he had "learned multitasking." Now, you have to understand that my husband is a wise and brilliant man. He often amazes me with the breadth and depth of his knowledge. But I have also lived with him a long time, so I asked him a little suspiciously what he meant by "multitasking."

His answer? "It means I can do two things at one time."

I have to confess that at that point I doubled over in laughter. Every woman I've told this story to has laughed just as hard. Two things at a time? Most women I know are accustomed to doing five or six or more tasks simultaneously. The problem, of course, is that many of us multitasking women have reached the point where we just can't do much more. Even if we could, our nervous systems couldn't take the strain. So many of us are burned out. We are falling behind. Because we've allowed our sense of self-worth to be connected to how much we cram into a day, we're feeling worse and worse. And because we take our information in sound bites and have little time to devote to deeper things, we are in danger of becoming shallow and superficial.

A pastor we know likes to talk about those who are willing to spend the time and energy to seriously study Scripture—or anything else, for that matter— as "deep-diving ducks." The sad truth is it is hard to be a deep-diving duck these days because such diving requires blocks of uninterrupted time, a commodity we just don't have.

So what's the answer to this warped time crunch? There's probably not much that you as an individual can do to change our culture—at least not in the short run. But you can definitely reduce the influence of this slice-and-dice society in your home. With some thought and planning and courage, plus patience and perseverance, you can learn to live more counterculturally, to rediscover what it means to live in God's time. For your own peace of mind and for your family's, you have to do it.

To start, take a minute to look around and evaluate the extent to which you have allowed our culture's hurry-up view of time drive you and rob you of your peace. And then, as an antidote, take another look at how *God* views time. After all, God created time in the first place, and his view of it has not changed, even if our view has. Here are a few hints about God and time that I have gleaned from Scripture and other reading:

- God's primary interests are eternal, and that's where he wants our focus too.

- God's love for us, and our value, doesn't depend on what we do.

- God wants us to take time as he gives it to us and not worry about today or tomorrow. He wants us to embrace each day and trust him to take care of us.

- God gives us the days of our lives for a purpose. Each moment is precious and not to be wasted.

- God often comes to us in ways that interrupt our plans. (His ways, remember, are not our ways.)

- God can be trusted to make things happen in his own time.

Once you have a clear understanding of how God views time, you can make some changes in your life that will help you live in his peace. Here are some practical suggestions.

First, try backing up a little, taking steps to simplify your schedule and your life. This may mean you need to drop some activities and get rid of some items. At the very least, think about what you're trading off to keep up with today's culture. Is all the stuff in your life really worth the time you must invest in it?

If you are a mom with children at home, simplifying may mean deciding to stay home instead of seeking outside work. I certainly applaud this effort and direct you to my book *The Stay-at-Home Mom* for ideas and support. But even if you're not prepared to make this decision or if it doesn't apply to you, you can probably find some ways to spread out your time a little by simplifying.

Another way to counter the dominant cultural hurry-up trend is to reduce your dependence on technology. Perhaps a better way to put it is to be sure technology works for you—not you for it. Because there is something almost hypnotic or even addictive about "toys" such as televisions and computers, you might need to make rules for yourself.

We've done that in our own home. For instance, we have chosen never to have a TV in our bedroom; we reserve that room for more restful activities. And though I do have a private e-mail address, I have chosen not to use e-mail to conduct my business—and I give my address only to a very few people.

It might help to rethink the ways you use technology and the numbers of electronic gadgets you use. What is truly helpful, what eats up valuable time, what adds to the background noise, what just gathers dust? In other words, would your life be more peaceful if some of your toys just weren't there? (If you can't bring yourself to turn it off or do without it, perhaps that very reluctance tells you something important.)

Anything you can do to reduce the number of choices you make in a day will help keep your household counterculturally calm. By all means, do whatever you can to reduce the onslaught of advertising you're exposed to. Invest in spam filters and subscribe to "no call" telephone lists. Toss or shred junk mail without even reading it. Even better, photocopy a form letter asking to be taken off advertisers' mailing lists and mail it to all companies that send you junk—if possible, in their own return envelope. By law, they have to honor your wishes.

Being intentional about your life goals, your purposes, and priorities is an important antidote to cultural chaos. If you set aside time to listen to God's specific call on your life and focus your energy on fulfilling that call, you'll be far less likely to waste your time on the cultural treadmill. You'll be living your life by conviction, not circumstance...and your life will be much more peaceful.

One of the most powerful ways to find peace is to remember to take your life a day at a time, just as God gives it to you. I like to think of this approach as "milk and honey" faith, the kind the Israelites had to practice to reach the Promised Land. (Yes, I know they often failed, but so do we—and God is faithful.) Or approach it as "Lord's Prayer" thinking: "Give us this day our daily bread."

That doesn't mean you shouldn't plan or look ahead to the future. An "organization" person like me would never say that! But you can save yourself a lot of stress and anxiety if you keep reminding yourself that what happens tomorrow is not entirely up to you. By all means, mark your calendar, draw up your to-do lists, anticipate and prepare for what might happen. But you will live a lot more peacefully if you expect surprises and determine to live as much by God's provision as by your well-laid plans.

OTTO'S MOTTO

Finish today today.

Whenever possible, allow for unhurried, unscheduled blocks of time. Remember that you control your schedule; it shouldn't control you. And you don't have to schedule *everything*. Resist the urge to chop every day into activity-sized chunks. Children and adults need time to just "be." Even the busiest schedule needs room for the unexpected, which is often the way we encounter God.

And though much needs to be done, try to resist the call of constant busyness. At very least, try not to be proud of your busyness! Elizabeth Prentiss puts it beautifully:

> If you could once make up your mind in the fear of God never to undertake more work of any sort than you can carry on calmly, quietly, without hurry or flurry, and the instant you feel yourself growing nervous, like one out of breath would stop and take breath, you would find this simple common sense rule doing for you what no prayers or tears could ever accomplish.

It helps to keep in touch with the natural rhythms God initiated from the beginning. With city lights and central heat and air, it's easy to lose track of the changes of seasons, the shifts of light from hour to hour, the phases of the moon, the cycle of night and day, the progression of the week. But our bodies and spirits are still aligned to those rhythms, and to ignore them is to invite unnecessary stress into our lives. So get out of doors whenever possible. Open windows when you can. Turn off the lights at a reasonable hour. Find time to look at the stars.

One of the most meaningful and peace-inducing experiences of my life is rediscovering the power of a true Sabbath, the weekly day of rest that was part of God's rhythms from the beginning. For several years now I have set aside every Wednesday as a Sabbath day. (My Sundays are so full of church activities and teaching that it's difficult to experience them as restful.) It took me approximately three years to accomplish the task of freeing up this day, convincing friends, associates, and myself that I really would not be doing business as usual on Wednesday. But since my "Sabbath" became established, I have seen a huge difference in my life. I don't answer the phone or go to meetings on Wednesdays. I don't schedule appointments. In fact, I don't have an agenda of any sort other than rest. I sleep a little later than usual. I dip into the books on my nightstand. I take walks or sit in the garden and pray as God leads me. This scheduled stillness has brought a silence to my soul that has helped me understand many things that I did not formerly understand. My friends have even commented on the change in me, pointing out that I have become more patient, more gentle, more thoughtful.

I'm not suggesting that you have to observe this kind of Sabbath for yourself. It may not be possible, at this time of your life to do so. With young kids at home, the idea of *15 minutes* alone may seem unattainable. Or you may have grown up with very legalistic Sabbath practices or just don't like the idea of "doing nothing" all day. And that's fine. Jesus made it clear that Sabbath was not meant to be an obligation, but an opportunity. So I would never attempt to dictate what your Sabbath experience should be—that's for you and the Lord to decide. All I can tell you is that the practice of Sabbath keeping has truly transformed my approach to the rest of my life.

However you decide to simplify your life and activities, I urge you to do whatever is necessary to become a deep-diving duck. Instead of paddling frantically in the spiritual shallows, spinning in smaller and smaller circles, take a deep breath and go deep. Take your family with you. Close the door, protect the time, turn off the noise, get rid of the stuff, take a break from slicing and dicing and multitasking, and dive.

Discover the depths of the Father's love, the fathomless gifts of his grace, the bottomless meaning of the work he calls you to. And the deep, abiding peace he wants to give you. Not as the world gives, but as he has planned for you from the beginning.

For this life and eternity—and for the home the Lord has given you—experience the blessings of a countercultural calm.

A Moment of
REFLECTION

1. What elements of your daily life tend to hurry you up and cause the most stress?

2. What specific steps could you take to calm down your household by adjusting the way you schedule your time?

3. Just for the exercise, list five aspects of your daily life you could eliminate in order to make your family's life more peaceful. What factors in yourself and your culture make it hard for you to do that?

DIVINE TIME

*God will always give you everything you need
to do his will, including time. Don't live in a rush.*

ELISABETH ELLIOT

ELEVEN

ORDERING YOUR WORLD

YOUR FAMILY MAY NOT TELL YOU. Your children may not know any better. Your husband may hesitate to bring it up. You yourself might not want to admit it.

But for everyone in your house—including you yourself—a peaceful home means an orderly home. Nobody really likes coming home to chaos. Nobody really likes searching frantically for lost things or wading through a collision course of stuff on the floor or searching for a place to sit among the stacks of unfolded laundry or not knowing when dinner will be ready.

We may get used to disorder and learn to live around it. Many of us do just that on a daily basis. And yet disorganization and disorder weigh down our spirits and rob us of peace—because we human beings were made for order. We were made in the image of our Creator God, who ordered the whole universe and called it good. And according to Genesis, the first task given to the very first man and woman was the task of "organizing" the animals by naming them. All through the Bible we find detailed and organized lists that indicate how God lived with his people—right down to the genealogy of Jesus. And that description of the perfect wife and mother in Proverbs 31 with her busy and productive lifestyle—isn't she the epitome of an orderly and organized woman?

Now, I'm the first to recognize that keeping things neat and orderly and organized isn't easy. I'm not naturally an organized person. Like everyone else, I came out of the womb lazy, and I also came out with a kind of flibbertigibbet temperament. I'm a bunny-trailer at heart; I love to skip and hop from this activity to that. I love to start things, but persevering and finishing well are skills I have had to learn. I used to hide my dirty dishes in the clothes dryer, and I lost my keys 23 times a day.

I can remember my four-year-old, brown-eyed, cherubic-faced daughter looking up at me one Sunday morning and saying to me, "Mommy, are we going to be late to church again?"

Just saying that grieves me. Why would any four-year-old need to ask such a question? Because we had walked in late so many times to church and to other places. And because even at that young age she knew the difference between a home that was a haven and one that was hectic and chaotic.

It took time and lots of effort and generous helpings of grace, but things have changed for us since then. Not only is my home now in order, but I know where everything is. I haven't lost my keys in years, and I rarely waste valuable time searching for something I've misplaced. I have an organizer-planner I carry with me everywhere I go, and it functions as my memory so that I almost never miss an appointment, and I'm rarely late. More importantly, I have much more time for relationships, for reaching out, for hearing the voice of God, for extending the love I feel from God to others. And it all started with a longing for order that I believe God built into even my flibbertigibbet nature—and my determination to create a haven of order for myself and the family I love so dearly.

I know you have said at one time or another, perhaps with a wistful sigh, "I've just got to get organized" or "I wish I had more order in my world." We all have this desire within us, and that was my starting place. I thought, *Why do I have this desire? Why do I constantly feel that if I could just get more organized, I would feel better?* Then I realized, *It's because God put it there. And it's there because he desires for me to live an orderly life. And if he created me for order, that means that being organized is something I really can do with his help.*

I believe that's true for you as well. God created you with your particular blend of natural and spiritual gifts and your particular temperament. He created you and your family as well, which is why you have a yearning for order and why you have a hard time feeling at peace in a messy, chaotic, and unpredictable household. Your need to get organized—even if it's a feeble whimper of discomfort or guilt—is there for a reason. It's part of the image of God within you. So I urge you to develop it. When you do, you'll discover your home is a far happier, more peaceful place.

Now, organization of the home is a big subject. It could take an entire book. In fact, I *have* written an entire book about it. (It's called *Get More Done in Less Time.*) So instead of repeating myself here and outlining a step-by-step approach to organizing your home, I'd like to set down some general organizing principles and techniques that have helped me and others over the years to establish a more satisfying environment.

The general approach can be summed up in four words: *identify, prepare, organize,* and *maintain.* If you take each of these steps in order, you'll greatly increase your chances of making a permanent change for the better.

First, identify your organizational problem. What are the big or little snags that annoy or irritate you on a regular basis or cause unrest in your home? Does your blood pressure rise every time you open your hall closet because piled up sweaters come tumbling out, or does your teenager constantly complain because he can't locate his favorite corduroy jacket? That's a good sign that your overcrowded, disorganized closet is a peace problem.

Are you sick to death of children who whine and stay underfoot while you are trying to cook dinner? That problem may call for reorganizing the way you organize your family's time.

Chances are, you can think of more than one problem that's causing you stress. Don't tackle them all at once or try to fix everything in a day! You'll become frustrated and be tempted to give up. Instead, start with the issue that bothers you most. (In God's time, you'll get to the others.) It may be a small thing that you can quickly fix, say a loose tile on the kitchen floor that you've just never gotten around to gluing back down. Or it may be a big issue, like coping with a chronically messy house. No matter what you choose, the next step is preparation.

Second, prepare to tackle the problem. Preparation is the key to all organization. Think about what you're going to do and what it will require. Think about how much time the project will take and how much time a day or week you can set aside. Do you have a whole day or week you can set aside for reorganization, or do you need to approach the problem in bite-sized chunks? (Either will work.) You may want to do some research, such as reading a book or two on organization. You may want to write out a plan. It's certainly a good idea to focus in on goals and priorities: What exactly do you want to accomplish and why? Write those goals down. Try to visualize the actual process of reorganization.

Most important, you need to steep the whole process in prayer. Ask God for strength and focus and a vision for a more orderly, peaceful life. Ask him for the power to persevere.

And then…get specific. Set a date to begin, and gather whatever materials you will need for your organization project. (Your research or planning will tell you this.) Buy or collect storage boxes and cartons. Find a filing cabinet. Measure that closet and order paint and new hardware for it. Try to anticipate what you will need and have it on hand so you won't be distracted in the middle of an organization problem and be tempted to quit.

If you're an active type who likes to get right down to business, you might find this preparation step frustrating. You want to step right in and whip that household into shape. But if you skip preparation, you're much more likely to bog down whenever the work hits a snag. On the other hand, if you're a more contemplative type, you may tend to get stuck in the planning stage, endlessly preparing for a job you never get around to.

Keeping your overall goals in mind can really help you at this point. You want your organizational efforts to work, so it pays to think ahead. It would be a shame to have your efforts sidetracked just because you ran out of storage boxes. It would also be a shame if you never got started.

Third, organize. To be honest, I've always found this part of the process fun. It's really a creative challenge. I love to dive into a problem and watch disorder gradually be banished by order. Piece by piece, items find a place. Clear space appears where piles of junk once lived. A workable schedule takes form. It almost seems like magic.

But organization takes a lot of energy, and it's not uncommon to run out of steam in the middle of a project. That's why it's so important to have a plan before you start. Big organizational projects require you to pace yourself and work in scheduled chunks. It's better to set aside an hour a day for organization, to stop at the end of that hour, and then to start again the next day than to work frenetically for hours, wear yourself out, and never quite finish.

"How do you eat an elephant?" I often ask women in my seminars. It's an old joke, but it always gets a laugh. And the answer, once the laughter has died down, is obviously "one bite at a time." The most time consuming organizational project becomes less formidable if you take it one "bite" at a time and persevere until you're finished. Break your chosen task into pieces if you have to. Tackle one closet at a time, or set your timer and tackle one closet for 15 minutes at a time. Set aside an hour a day to fine-tune your organization system or file away the papers piled around your office. At the end of each day's allotted time, stop. Tuck your supplies away somewhere if you can, take out the trash you've generated, and go on about your business. Just be sure you show up for the next day's "bite."

If you persevere in this matter, you'll be finished organizing before you know it. But without the final step, maintenance, it all could be for naught.

Fourth, maintain. This is the step most of us would like to skip. While organizing and reorganizing can be fun, maintenance can feel like drudgery. What do I mean by maintenance? Simply the day-in, day-out business of getting things done.

I'll never forget a day when our cupboards were almost bare and my grocery list was even longer than usual. Going to market is never my favorite task, but on this day it really felt like a chore. But I persevered. I pushed my cart up and down aisles, compared prices, made choices, and checked off items. I steered the cart through the checkout line, gulped at the bill but paid it, loaded the groceries in the car, and then carted them all home, where I proceeded to unload the bags and put everything away. I weeded out old items from the refrigerator and wiped down the shelves. I made the hamburger into individual patties and placed them in freezer bags. I washed salad greens for the week and tucked them away in the crisper. I cut up onions and garlic and vegetables to have them ready for my planned meals. I even prepared healthy snacks and placed them in the front of the refrigerator.

When it was all finished, my pantry and refrigerator looked beautiful—neat, organized, and bursting with abundance. I had done a wonderful job. But all I could think as I admired my handiwork was: "All right now—nobody eat!"

Maintenance, above all, means coming to terms with the reality that no matter how hard you work at a given task in your home, you're probably going to have to do it over and over. The moments when your house is completely clean, the washing is completely done, and every item on your grocery list is checked off will be few and short-lived. People are going to eat. You will have to shop and chop and stock. And then you will need to do it all over again. If you have teenagers, you might have to do it several times a day!

Where organization takes creative effort and invigorating energy, maintenance requires discipline and perseverance. But it's the maintenance that makes the real difference in making your home a more peaceful, satisfying place to live. The magic of order really resides in the patient act of maintenance.

I have found it helps to write acts of maintenance on my calendar, especially until they become a habit. It's encouraging to check off a to-do item, and the very act of scheduling guards against forgetting. I even know women who jog their memory and spark their enthusiasm by setting specific maintenance goals—for instance, "I will maintain my new morning schedule by setting the breakfast table in the evening and laying out morning clothes every day for a month."

The power of habit on the human psyche can be a big help here. Experts say it takes a minimum of six weeks to make a new habit, but a habit, once established, is hard to break. That means if you can persevere in new practices of maintenance for a month and a half, force of habit will likely keep you going after that. Involving everyone in the house in a new routine can also help. Success breeds success.

I have found that the process of maintenance also means periodically reevaluating my organizational systems—my planner notebook, my files, my closets, my storage system—to see what is working and what isn't working. My planner, which I've always called my daybook, has been a work in progress for many years. So have my files. I'm constantly adding and taking away categories, weeding out files and sections, putting items in long-term storage or throwing away outdated items. The result is that organizational systems I put into practice long ago still essentially work for me, and I rarely have to start over.

A Moment of
REFLECTION

1. Name three specific organizational "elephants" that add stress to your life at home. Which is the biggest problem?

2. Write out a plan for tackling one single organizational obstacle in your life. Schedule a time to begin.

3. Why do you think maintenance is such a challenge for many people? Under what circumstances do you tend to let things slide?

Simplify! Simplify!

Every step you take to simplify your life can pay dividends in terms of the peace of your home.

- Group items on surfaces in trays or baskets so you can leave the surfaces clear.

- Make a house rule: Whenever something new comes in, something old should come out. This applies to clothing, toys, electronics, whatever. Unless it's an heirloom or you have another use for it, throw it away or give it to charity.

- Make another rule: Put it back where you got it from.

- Never say yes or no immediately to a request for your time. Ask for 24 hours to think about it.

- Work toward coordinating your wardrobe around a single flattering color scheme so that everything works with everything else.

- Save money and time on cards by printing up a set of simple, personalized stationery and using it for congratulations, condolences, and thank-you notes.

- Invest in a few large rolls of solid-colored wrapping paper that will work for almost any occasion. Personalize it if you wish with ribbons or even felt-tip pens.

- Put all your "to read" material—catalogs, newsletters, and so on—into a totable file to take with you on errands. Use any waiting time you have to read. In your file include a pen, a few note cards, and some stamps.

TWELVE

ONE SMALL STEP

Has this whole explanation of the organization process seemed a little theoretical? Let's try a more specific—and very familiar—example.

Say, for instance, that the organizational problem you've identified in your house involves clutter and mess. You spend most of your time picking up stuff in your home, and yet you never seem to make a dent. Clothes are draped over your bedroom chair because there's not enough room in your dressers and your closet is stuffed. There's barely enough space on the kitchen counter to prepare dinner. You have to watch your feet as you walk anywhere in the house to avoid stepping on children's toys or your husband's sports equipment or the shoes you took off when you came home to your particular holy ground.

Clearly, clutter and disorganization are a peace problem for you. But if you apply the identify/prepare/organize/maintain plan to it, you can conquer the clutter problem once and for all in your home. I'm going to briefly outline how you might approach it. (Again, for more detail instructions, I refer you to *Get More Done in Less Time*.)

Once you've identified your clutter problem and decided that it's the biggest peace-eater in your life at the moment, you can prepare to tackle it. Even though you may be longing to get at the mess and get rid of it, set aside some time to think and pray about your clutter problem. Specifically ask God to give you the courage to move beyond clutter and disorganization and to make your home a refuge.

Assess your time situation. Would it be possible for you to block off a week or so to completely reorganize your house? That would be great, though you can accomplish the same thing by working in small planned chunks over a period of months—while your kids are in Mother's Day Out, for example. If you opt to tackle the problem a bit at a time, consider whether there is a corner of your garage, an extra closet, or an area in a room where you can store organizational supplies while you are in the process of reworking.

Another question you might ask is whether you need some help. Is your husband or teenage son available to cart off heavy items? Many women find that the process of simplifying and reorganizing requires a lot of decision making, and the moral support and extra pair of hands can be a lifesaver. Perhaps you and a friend could trade off help with organization chores.

OTTO'S MOTTO

It's not what you do that makes you tired.
It's what you *don't* do!

Take a little time to decide your strategy. Will you tackle one room at a time or go for the whole house? Since the clutter problem in your room is really rooted in a disorganized closet, perhaps the best place to start is the bedroom closet or your dresser drawers.

Take a minute to gather the supplies you'll need for reorganization. For a closet reorganization, I suggest large cardboard boxes or plastic bins, a box of large heavy-duty trash bags, and a place to store items you want to keep but don't need on an everyday basis.

Having made preparations, you're ready to put on your grubbies and tackle the issue. Here's a strategy: Begin with a surface cleaning in the room. This means gathering up all the extraneous clutter *without* taking the time to organize. Take the biggest box you can find and put in it everything that is out of place or that doesn't *have* a place. Take the box with you as you work your way around the room. Throw in anything that doesn't belong where it is— dirty clothes, clean clothes, shoes, toys, books, whatever. If you fill the box up, pull out another and keep going. You might want to stack loose papers or those pesky piles of paper in a separate, smaller box or bag. Keep a garbage bag with you as well for anything that obviously needs to be thrown away, but don't put any effort at this point into deciding whether something's trash or not. Instead, concentrate on getting everything looking clear and neat.

When you're finished clearing the space, throw away the garbage bag, tuck your boxes out of sight and do a quick cleaning. Dust the flat surfaces that have miraculously appeared. Run the vacuum over traffic areas. But don't worry about getting the place really clean; just take care of anything obvious. Then look around you and enjoy the lift you get from the sight of what your home can look like *all* the time.

Once you've done a surface cleaning, it's time to tackle all those out-of-place objects you put in the box. Take three trash bags (or three more boxes) into the room you've just surface cleaned. If you wish, label them "throw away," "give away," and "put away." Then start in on your collection of out-of-place items. Pick up each item and make a decision about it before picking up the next. Everything in the box either goes into one of the three bags or into its proper place in the room.

Once you have sorted through those boxes, go through the entire room—and the entire house—the same way. Every item should be either thrown away, given away, or put away properly. If you don't need it on a regular basis, I suggest you store it in a numbered box in your garage or attic and record the contents of each box on an index card.

Be sure to dispose of the "throw away" bags as quickly as you fill them up so you won't be tempted to change your mind. The same goes for the "give away" bag. When you fill it up, take it straight to your car for drop-off at a charitable organization. When the put-away bag gets full, take it around the house and put items in their place or in storage boxes.

What about those closets and drawers? The basic strategy is the same—and again, it might be wise to tackle them first. Pull out the contents of the closet or take one drawer at a time. Sort the items into "throw away," "give away," and "put away." If necessary, rearrange the storage space to be more efficient—use drawer dividers or new closet hardware. Then put back only what makes sense for that particular storage space in that particular room—items you use in that room on a regular basis.

And then...you're through. You've taken the last bite of that elephant, and you're ready to lick your lips and smile, knowing you can use this same method anytime, anywhere for the rest of your life.

Don't you feel more peaceful already?

A Moment of REFLECTION

1. No need for questions here. Just do it!

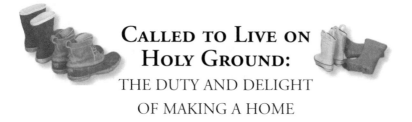

CALLED TO LIVE ON HOLY GROUND:
THE DUTY AND DELIGHT
OF MAKING A HOME

As a woman...

> *My first duty is to love the Lord with all my heart and soul and might, and to love my neighbor as myself.*

> *My greatest delight is to bask in the Lord's love and enjoy his loving presence.*

As one God has blessed with a home...

> *My duty is to create and maintain a space that honors God, nurtures the spirit, enhances growth, and ministers to others.*

> *My delight is to enjoy the home I've shaped and the sense of accomplishment that comes from obedience.*

As a wife...

> *My duty is to respect my husband, to submit to him when agreement is not possible, and to help him do what God has called him to do.*

> *My delight is to live as an intimate ally with the man God has given me and to enjoy his protection and care.*

As a mother...

> *My duty is to grow in the Lord and to help my children develop the character, knowledge, self-discipline, and practical skills they need to contribute to society and further God's kingdom.*

> *My delight is for everyone in the household to grow in wisdom, in stature, and in favor with God and man.*

As a follower of Christ...

> *My duty is to do everything in my home to the glory of God.*

> *My delight is to see the world changed because of what happens on this holy ground.*

THIRTEEN

CULTIVATING PEACEFUL RELATIONSHIPS

I DON'T LIKE PEOPLE," the young woman told me on the phone. "They frustrate me."

I had to smile at her honesty. We all have times when we just don't care for people. They bother us. They get on our nerves. They disturb our peace. And yes, that applies to your adorable, beloved husband and your precious children and anyone else who shares your life in and out of your home.

Relationship issues are the biggest contributors to a stressful household. The people we encounter daily often frustrate us. They get in our way. They contradict us—or, just as maddening, they give us the silent treatment. They leave hair in the bathtub or play the stereo too loudly or don't appreciate our efforts to help them. In one way or another, they disturb our peace. In our more honest moments, we have to admit we do the same to them.

And here's another truth: No matter how soothing the ambience of your home, no matter how controlled you keep your schedule or how neat and orderly you keep the place, your home won't feel like a haven unless the people who live there are at peace with one another.

This is not news to you. You know how uncomfortable a conflicted home can be. So how can you make sure that relational peace happens in your home?

The short answer is: You can't.

Because everyone who lives in your home is a sinner, including you, it's a given that you will hurt each other and annoy each other from time to time. Everyone in your household will fall short of the glory of God in this respect. There will be disagreements…and discomfort…and perhaps the occasional knock-down, drag-out fight. There will be times when the residents of a household are not at peace with one another.

And there's yet another reality to consider. No matter how much you desire peace and want it for your home, you can't achieve it by yourself. It takes two people to have a relationship. So you can do everything possible to live harmoniously and still have problems if the other person won't cooperate.

The apostle Paul recognizes this reality when he counsels, "If possible, *so far as it depends on you,* be at peace with all men" (Romans 12:18, emphasis added). Note that little phrase "so far as it depends on you." You can't force another person to work out a disagreement with you or forgive a slight or stop driving you crazy by leaving dirty socks on the floor. You can physically compel small children to do what you want. But as any mother who has ever broken up a squabble will testify, you can't coerce even little ones into adopting peaceful attitudes.

Does that mean there is no point in trying? Of course not. There is much you *can* do "so far as it depends on you" to promote peace in your household. Some approaches are easier than others, some take time, and all require some discipline. But all, with God's help and some maturity, are within your grasp. Here are ten of the most important things you can do to promote relational peace in your home:

1. *You can pray.* This is just a basic. Be sure and keep those who share your home in your prayers. Pray for each person specifically. Pray also for God's help with your own attitudes and actions and for the Spirit of peace to reign in your home.

2. *You can observe God's order.* Order, remember, was God's idea, and it's his gift to us to help us live peacefully. But we have to do it his way, and that's where many of us get stuck. We tend to rebel against the way he has chosen to organize the family.

The book of Colossians makes it clear: "Wives, be subject to your husbands, as is fitting in the Lord. Husbands, love your wives and do not be embittered against them. Children, be obedient to your parents in all things, for this is well-pleasing to the Lord. Fathers, do not exasperate your children, so that they will not lose heart" (Colossians 3:18-21). This passage sums up precisely the roles God has established for the various members of the family: wives submit, husbands love, children obey, and parents don't exasperate. But Ephesians 5:21 zeroes in on the overall context for the plan— one that applies even to households without husbands, wives, or children: "Be subject to one another in the fear of Christ."

The point is, our relationships will be a lot more peaceful when we get our authority issues straight—beginning with the reality that God is the one in charge. Power struggles are part of being human, but we who are followers of Christ are called to something higher. We are called to give up our one-upmanship, our wrestling for dominance, and follow his direction.

It's no secret that this issue is controversial even among Jesus' followers and that misuse of these passages has been the cause of much relational pain. And yet I know in my own life that when I try to bring my own hardheaded, power-hungry spirit in line with God's relational order, my heart and my household become a lot more peaceful. When I practice respectful (not toxic) submission to the Lord and to my husband, when I expect obedience from my children but try to avoid exasperating them, and, most of all, when I make obedience to God's Word and the Holy Spirit's prompting a priority in my own life, I am doing what I can to keep relational peace…and I reap the benefits as well.

3. *You can adjust your attitude.* This will make such a difference in your household. Attitudes of cheerfulness, gentleness, contentment,

and flexibility tend to be contagious; they are the most effective way to set the "thermostat" in your home and keep things relationally calm.

I realize such attitudes are not always easy to come by, especially when I'm feeling stressed. To a certain point, we can choose our attitudes, but I'm not one of those people who will counsel you to "fake it until you make it." I believe the only reliable way to cultivate peaceful attitudes is to rely on God's guidance and strength to develop the fruit of the Spirit as outlined in Galatians 5:22-23: "love, joy, peace, patience, kindness, goodness, faithfulness, gentleness, self-control."

One attitude to be especially diligent about is the all-too-human tendency to take those you love and live closely with for granted. You know how easy this is to do. Even when familiarity doesn't breed contempt, it can generate a careless attitude toward the people we see every day, even the people we love most. That's when we find ourselves forgetting to show respect, courtesy, or self-control. We become careless about our language—saying hurtful things simply because we don't bother to control ourselves. We can be careless about our looks, living in sloppy sweats that do little to bless our husbands. We make excuses about losing our temper with children or teenagers.

We know better. We know that our families deserve *better* than our company manners—more courtesy and consideration than we would give to strangers. But we forget so easily.

When I was researching the Jewish concept of *shalom bayit,* or peace in the home, I found a wonderful quote by a contemporary Orthodox rabbi that shows how this can work. "If you say you can't control yourself," he said, "that you are that mad—then imagine if the President of the United States were to walk into your home at that very moment. Surely then you would speak in a restrained and dignified manner. You can control yourself. You just have to be properly motivated to think of your spouse and your children as important as any visiting dignitary."*

---

* As quoted in "Shalom Bayit—Peace in the Home," Congregation Shir Hadash Rabbi's Corner, October 18, 2001, http://www.shirhadash.org/rabbi/011018-shalom-bayit.html, accessed September 2003.

What a wonderful thought—and what a builder of family peace. We don't need to be stiff and formal with our families. But remembering to treat the people we see every day with as much respect as we would treat people we meet outside the home will do a lot to keep our lives peaceful.

4. *You can tame your tongue.* It's not a secret that many women love to talk—and that many of us get in trouble that way. Words usually come easier for us. We are more likely to use them as weapons when we are frustrated. And our higher voices can easily become strident and annoying. For most of us women, therefore, learning to discipline our speech is an important step toward keeping peace at home and making our home a refuge.

One of the most effective ways I have found to discipline my tongue is to show more than I tell. This approach is really counterintuitive to me. My natural tendency is to explain exactly how something should be done and then expect people to do what I told them. But the truth is that most people learn better from example and gentle correction than they do from words. Your children learn more about running a household from watching you do chores—and having you watch and correct them—than they do by listening to your lectures. Your husband is likely to "hear" your love more loudly when you show it by rubbing his back or ironing his shirts or listening to his music with him.

I'm not saying you should never use words to outline what needs to be done or to express your love or to explain your point of view or just to connect with the people you care about. Language, after all, is a gift from God, and God wants us to use his gifts to his glory. But those of us to whom words come easily can live a lot more peacefully by learning to use those words carefully.

What can you do when your need to talk is greater than the willingness of your family to listen? That's an issue for some women who thrive on verbal communication but live with more silent types—usually men! But that's precisely why I recommend that you cultivate outside relationships with other women, with your mentors and sisters. Part of the relief of being with other women is the pure joy of talking a mile a minute. And once you've gotten your "talking fix," you'll find it far easier to control the flow of words at home.

Another important and effective way to tame the tongue is to practice speaking softly. Proverbs 15:1 confirms this: "A gentle answer turns away wrath, but a harsh word stirs up anger." Not only is it possible to communicate effectively without being loud and strident, but a firm but gentle request will usually solicit a better response than a harsh one.

I realize that some people and some households are naturally louder than others. After all, I'm half Italian, and I'm not a quiet person by nature. In fact, I remember a time when Erin, a dear friend and a "daughter of my heart," approached me timidly about an "argument" she had overheard between me and Anissa. I was mystified; I couldn't remember any argument. Then I realized that Anissa and I had just been having one of our typically loud discussions. We hadn't been angry at all, but it had sounded that way to soft-spoken Erin.

Even in a family where noisy, lively discussions are the norm, however, a dose of gentleness can keep loud from becoming irritating and those lively discussions from deteriorating into free-for-alls. If you're unsure whether your voice becomes strident, try tape-recording some of your everyday conversations. And whether you speak loudly or softly, try to avoid nagging. This is a challenge for many of us who like to get things done. When people don't respond to our requests as quickly as we would like, we are inclined to remind them...and remind them again, usually with a distinct edge to our voice.

The fact is, nobody likes to be nagged. The book of Proverbs says that "a constant dripping on a day of steady rain and a contentious woman are alike" (Proverbs 27:15). And because nagging is so unpleasant, most people either tune it out or respond in anger—which means it rarely provides the results we want. In fact, nagging usually has the opposite effect. Those who are under our authority—our children—become conditioned not to obey the first time. And those who are *not* under our authority—such as husbands and adult housemates—either ignore us or fight back.

How do you overcome a habit of nagging? With children, I believe the best way is to instill a policy of "I'll tell you one time." Make it clear that you expect to be obeyed the first time you tell them something and that if you need to tell them a second time there will be consequences. Then follow through with the consequences. If you persist with this policy, I can guarantee you'll cut back on your need to nag.

With others, and I'm thinking of husbands in particular, overcoming nagging is more a matter of overcoming our expectation that the other person should do things our way and on our schedule. I have observed that many men (a certain David Otto comes to mind) like to think things through before acting, and this means that they may be slower to respond than their women (such as a certain Donna Otto) prefer. In these cases, the best strategy might be just to wait a little. Other ideas might include putting a request in writing instead of speaking it or rethinking whether the request is even necessary. Whatever the situation, if you keep in mind that nagging is usually counterproductive, you'll turn up the level of peace in your home.

5. *You can keep short accounts.* This may or may not be a problem for you, but it's hard to maintain a peaceful household when you are nursing a grudge or stewing over an offhand remark. One of the most peaceful practices I know is to develop the habit of not letting disagreements fester. If you've had a fight with someone you care about or taken offense or something, give yourself a little time to cool off and then go to the other person and try to settle the matter in a gentle, constructive manner.

6. *You can pick your battles.* There are some issues that are truly important and worth going to the mat over. Being a peacemaker has never meant sweeping issues under the rug or avoiding trouble. It does not mean "peace at any price." Even Jesus, the Prince of

Peace, was willing to face conflict or even cause it when necessary. In family life, as in the rest of life, some things really are worth fighting about—but not nearly as many as some people believe. Some issues need to be faced, but others are best handled with benign neglect—and your life will be a lot more peaceful if you recognize which is which.

My husband is an incredibly patient man. He is not easily riled. But I'll never forget a time when he became so annoyed with me that he literally banged his fist down. I grew up in a very large city where driving could be a challenge and where turning left can either mean long delays or risking your life in a mad dash through a yellow light. As a result, I've always planned my expeditions to avoid as many left turns as possible. The problem was, when David was driving, I tended to "help" him by constantly telling him where to turn—and David has no trepidation at all about turning left.

One day when we were driving together, I gave him another set of "right turn" directions, and he finally lost patience. "Donna," he said, putting his fist down forcefully on the steering wheel, "does it really matter?"

The answer, of course, was that it really didn't. David was driving. I trusted him. And the truth was, whether we turned left or right just wasn't that important. Since then, before raising an issue with David, I've tried to learn to ask myself, "Does it really matter?" Much of the time, I find, the answer is no.

I have come to believe that the two most potent peace-killers are the need to be right and the need to assess blame. We all have that, don't we? We feel we can't let go of an argument until we have won—or at least made our point. And we feel the need to determine who was at fault, though the fault usually rests with both people. But this is another aspect to picking our battles. W will live a lot more peacefully if we can set aside our need to be right and to pinpoint a culprit.

7. *You can be sensitive to each person's temperament and needs.* Relational sparks often fly simply because people are different.

Gender differences, differences in temperaments, even differences in body clocks can result in misunderstandings or just plain irritation—as any "morning person" who has tried to communicate with a "night person" first thing in the morning will understand. Extroverts sometimes have trouble understanding why introverts can be so "unfriendly" and withdrawn, while introverts grow weary of the extrovert's need for interaction.

How can you strive for relational peace in the face of such differences? By doing what you can to know and accept one another. Educating yourself about human differences and temperaments can help, but intentionally observing each other, carefully listening, and prayerfully considering one another are just as important.

OTTO'S MOTTO

No serious conversation after 10:30 P.M.

Keep in mind that it's not always our differences that lead to friction between us. Have you ever been really annoyed by a particular trait in another person, only to realize you dislike that same trait in yourself? One wife told me that she and her husband both tended to be a little prickly and oversensitive when they were tired, and they ended up "prickling" each other. And many a mother has found herself coming down too hard on a child who displays a trait—shyness, recklessness, or a tendency to overeat—she herself has battled.

Making your home a place of peace involves so much more than avoiding conflict. It's also a matter of opening our arms to one another, appreciating one another, accepting each other just as we are and not requiring each other to squeeze into narrow molds. One of the things that makes home *home* is that sense of freedom to be exactly who we are. That doesn't mean we're all free to say whatever we think or do whatever we want when we want to do it—

because living in relationship means giving up some of that freedom for the sake of the other person. And yet a home where people strive to understand and accept each other and rejoice in each other's unique qualities is one that truly speaks a message of peace.

8. *You can lead your children in the ways of peace.* I believe this is one of the most important steps you can take as a mother to make your home a peaceful haven. Your influence on your children is greater than you probably imagine. Teaching them to live peacefully and lovingly with others is a wonderful gift you can give the world.

The earlier you begin, of course, the easier this will be. From the time your children are small, train them to obey the first time—without argument—and enforce their obedience. Establish consistent routines that help them feel secure—this, too, fosters peace instead of chaos. Teach and enforce courtesy and show children how and why to serve others.

One of the most valuable ways you can teach children relational peace is to promote activities that make children feel a part of that family, that install a sense of "we." Family traditions can do this—anything from "We always go to Grandma's for Thanksgiving" to "We always sing silly songs together in the car." Working together on common projects such as cleaning the yard or planting a garden has a similar effect. And casting rules of behavior in a "we" mode—"We always help each other in our house"—is an effective way to build a sense of peaceful unity.

It's a given that if you have children in the home, you will also have a certain amount of bickering and squabbles. David and I raised an only child, and even we were not immune from the discord that comes with immaturity. So it's helpful to keep in mind that peace in the home is a learning process for everyone. None of us gets it right all the time.

9. *You can make space for silence and rest.* Anyone who has spent time with small children knows they become grumpy when they are

tired and overstimulated. This is true for big people too. In fact, much of the bickering and unpleasantness in your home may come from people who are either wired or tired or hungry—or all three.

Remember, our dominant culture is geared toward nonstop stimulation and activity, and our nervous systems weren't meant to withstand that much "noise." Even when you're not aware of being worn down, the pressures of our culture may make you and those you love more irritable, less patient, and a lot less peaceful.

What is the antidote? A little peace and quiet. Every person in your household needs some quiet time and emotional space to rest and recover and get over the grumpies.

I learned this most dramatically when I was a stay-at-home mother with a small child. Being alone all day with a toddler was a stimulating experience in many ways, but it left me hungry for adult conversation. So the minute that David walked in the door, I would tend to bombard him with talk—not nagging or unpleasantness, just a deluge of the words I had stored up during those days when most of my conversations consisted of "no."

The problem, of course, was that David had spent his day having adult conversations, and he was simply worn out with words. He would respond to my deluge reluctantly, if at all. I grew testy. David grew grumpy. Anissa, sensing the tension, would respond with her own forms of misbehavior. And none of us felt very peaceful.

It took some long talks (not right after work) and a heaping helping of the Lord's grace, but David and I finally figured out how to short-circuit this maddening scenario. We called it "home free," and it made a dramatic difference in our peace level. Simply put, I gave my weary husband the gift of space and quiet. For half an hour after he got home, he was "home free." I gave him a kiss and a hug and a cheeseboard with cheese and slices of apple, and then I left him alone. He would change his clothes and regroup a little. Then, when he emerged, he was ready to listen to me.

In order for this to work, I had to learn to make space for Anissa and me as well. I learned to make "quiet times" part of our routine—both together and apart. Even at an early age, she was able to understand that there was a time for boisterous behavior and a time for quiet, a time for sharing and a time for being alone.

Over time, I have grown to understand my own needs to be "home free" from time to time and have come to recognize the relational benefits of scheduling quiet time for myself. Because I am naturally gregarious and love to be in the midst of activity, this was something I had to learn. And, of course, when I had small children at home (for a while, David's sister's children lived with us), finding even a moment of quiet was sometimes a challenge. Today, when I have a busy office in my home, quiet is still something I have to be intentional about. But I almost never regret the time I set aside for rest and silence. My relationships are always better when I've had some down time.

10. *Finally, you can be a relational peacemaker in your home by majoring in grace.* That's what God does. All through history, his response to our failure to live peacefully and righteously has been to correct us, teach us, and give us another chance. Again and again we have failed to live the way he wanted us to, have rebelled against him and his ways, have offended his holy nature. And again and again God has responded with amazing grace.

Grace, by definition, is undeserved favor. It's giving good things to people who have done little or nothing to merit them. It's offering second…and third…and more chances to people who can't guarantee they've learned their lesson.

"For of His fullness we have all received and *grace upon grace*" (John 1:16, emphasis added).

Don't you just love that phrase "grace upon grace"? Whenever I hear it, I think of a time years ago, during a family Thanksgiving celebration, when my nephew Jason stood by my elbow asking for "lots" of whipped cream on his pumpkin pie.

"Wait for Aunt Donna," I told him. Then I began piling the rich, fluffy cream higher and higher on his slice of pie—spoonful upon spoonful of delicious white stuff. Jason's eyes grew bigger and bigger as I piled on the cream until it plopped off the edges of the pie.

"Jason," I told my nephew, "if you trust God, he will give you that kind of blessing, that kind of grace."

Grace upon grace—piled up, impossibly generous—that's what God, who is perfect, extends to every one of us. So how can we, who know we don't even come close to perfect, fail to extend such grace to the imperfect, beloved people who share our homes?

Forgiveness is an important part of grace. When we are hurt, our natural human response is to hurt back—and being hurt is a built-in part of relationships. But relational experts stress that learning to forgive is one of the chief components of living happy, peaceful lives, and learning to forgive the people we live with is absolutely necessary to maintaining a peaceful home. After all, who wants to come home to an atmosphere of resentment and stale anger?

Is forgiveness easy? You know the answer to that! But the Scriptures make it clear that forgiveness is not only possible; it's a requirement for God's people. "Be kind to one another, tenderhearted, forgiving each other, just as God in Christ also has forgiven you" (Ephesians 4:32).

As long as we live in this fallen world, we won't achieve perfect relational harmony. But with God's gift of grace, we can always keep moving forward in peace.

A Moment of
REFLECTION

1. Of the ten strategies listed in this chapter, which one is the simplest for you to implement? Which is the hardest?

2. Think about a typical day in your household. Is there a particular time or circumstance when relational peace becomes a problem?

3. What personalities or temperaments—or specific people in your life—do you find it harder to live peacefully with? Do any of the suggestions in this chapter make peace easier with these people?

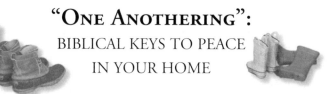

"ONE ANOTHERING":
BIBLICAL KEYS TO PEACE
IN YOUR HOME

*H*ow family members treat one another is a key ingredient in a peaceful home. Here are some verses from the Bible on peaceful relationships:

- *Be devoted to one another in brotherly love; give preference to one another in honor (Romans 12:10).*

- *Let us not judge one another anymore, but rather determine this—not to put an obstacle or a stumbling block in a brother's way (Romans 14:13).*

- *Accept one another, just as Christ also accepted us to the glory of God (Romans 15:7).*

- *Greet one another with a holy kiss (Romans 16:16). Note: Hugs count too!*

- *Through love serve one another (Galatians 5:13).*

- *Be subject to one another in the fear of Christ (Ephesians 5:21).*

- *Let the word of Christ richly dwell within you, with all wisdom teaching and admonishing one another with psalms and hymns and spiritual songs (Colossians 3:16).*

- *Encourage one another and build up one another (1 Thessalonians 5:11).*

- *Encourage one another day after day, as long as it is called Today, so that none of you will be hardened by the deceitfulness of sin (Hebrews 3:13).*

- *Fervently love one another, from the heart (1 Peter 1:22)*

- *Be hospitable to one another without complaint (1 Peter 4:9).*

- *If we walk in the Light, as He Himself is in the Light, we have fellowship with one another (1 John 1:7).*

FOURTEEN

THE GIFT OF
A LOVING HOME

IT WAS A DARK LITTLE HOUSE, furnished with hand-me-downs; and with two growing boys, the five rooms were barely adequate. The small windows didn't let in much light. The décor consisted of a few crocheted afghans and pictures of the boys on the wall—not much more—and everything was a little threadbare. Money was chronically tight not only because the mother had chosen to be a stay-at-home mom, but also because her cancer treatment first showed up during a brief period when the husband was between jobs and without insurance.

If you didn't know better, you would think that home would be a depressing place to visit. It wasn't. Children and adults alike enjoyed spending time there. The boys were friendly, boisterous, obedient, and cheerful. The father worked long hours—two jobs, plus a correspondence course—but he made time for his children and went out of his way to do little things for his wife. And she was a happy soul who babysat for the neighbors' children and helped her husband with his studies and practiced hard to learn sign language so she could be involved with her church's deaf ministry.

That home was a joyful place to be—not because of the décor or the ambience, not because that home had an absence of problems, but because love lived there. It filled the air; it seemed to be woven into the carpet. And no one ever visited that house without feeling that it was a wonderful place to be.

Love lives here. Can you think of a more wonderful description for any home? No matter what the place looks like, no matter how much or how little it costs or how it's furnished, if love fills the rooms, that home will be holy ground for those who live there and those who visit. Love is the spark that warms a home and makes it truly a haven. It's the bond that makes family roles—husband, wife, parent, child, leader, servant—more than legalistic job descriptions. It's the creative force that transforms a collection of walls and floors into a place where people grow and learn and serve each other. A sense of peace and calm may make a house livable, but love, more than anything else, makes it a home.

Though desirable, love sometimes seems hard to come by and tricky to keep alive. Why do our homes clang with conflict or ring with emptiness instead of glow with love? I believe the answer is that we can, out of selfishness, cut ourselves off from the love God gives us so freely, and in the process the love that is meant to warm our hearts and draw us together in him is absent in our lives and home.

That was certainly true for me when I was growing up. In retrospect, I know my parents loved me, but I can't really say I grew up in a loving home.

My mother, as an unmarried teenager bucking her father's disapproval, made a tremendous sacrifice just to bring me into this world. She worked long hours at a turkey plant to support me, and then she endured 13 years of a loveless marriage so I would have a home. As an adult, I can look back and see love in her fierce protectiveness, her insistence that I learn household skills, her occasional splurges on a play downtown for the two of us—just as I see love in my father's insistence on marrying my mother once he found out about me, his pride in me as his daughter, and his insistence that I learn real job skills so I could support myself in the world.

I can appreciate all those actions now as evidence of my parents' real, if flawed, love. I have even learned to be grateful for the gifts each of them gave me. And yet, looking back, I feel acutely the lack of what I think of as a loving home. Instead, when I envision the home of my childhood, I see a place that is lonely and barren.

How can you have real love and still have a loveless home? In my case, it was partly because God's kind of love was never part of the mix. My parents' love for me and my brother was fierce, protective, well-meaning—but God's brand of patient, kind, unselfish love was something they just did not understand. In addition, neither of my parents had ever learned to express or communicate their love effectively. A home with a loving, affirming atmosphere was a gift they did not know how to give.

Showing love, you see, is different from *feeling* love. And actually *communicating* love—expressing our devotion in ways that actually make the other person feel valued—can be tricky. I learned the hard way that creating and maintaining a loving home involve much more than simply caring about those around you. Just as important is learning to express that love to others in ways that they can hear and understand and feel deeply.

Simply put, a home where love lives is a home where the message of love comes across clearly. It's a home where the presence of love is felt, where everyone in the house is confident of being valued and cherished. It's where love is communicated by words, touch, actions, little gestures and large ones, little tokens and lavish gifts. Most important, it's where love is spoken in a language everyone can understand.

At a very basic level, a loving house is one that *feels* loving to those who live there. And yes, I know we've said that love is more than a feeling. But when God's kind of love is employed with energy and imagination, good feelings almost certainly result—for both givers and receivers of expressed love. Even more important, there will be a deep sense of *knowing*—a heart-deep understanding that, no matter what else goes on in a household, love is being shared and lived out.

There may be disagreements in such a house, even the occasional knock-down, drag-out fight. Husbands and wives and parents and children and friends and guests will rub each other the wrong way from time to time. But a strong sense of shared love can insulate a home from some of the friction. It's like a savings account that buffers against unexpected deficits.

Even more important, when we work at communicating real love to one another, we become conduits for the love of God here on earth.

That's what we all want, of course. It's the most basic definition of a home that is holy ground—it's a place where love does its redeeming work on the most intimate level. It's where love is learned, where love is acted out, where love is shared, where love is understood. Such a home is a gift both to those who live there and all who encounter it.

But how do you create such a loving atmosphere in a home? I'd like to suggest a few basic principles that have really helped me understand how to create the kind of loving home atmosphere I never had as a child—a home where love thrives.

The first principle is basic: *Love thrives on gifts that fit.* I'm not just talking about shirts and sweaters here—although I hope you give the right size to those you love. I'm talking about observing the people you live with, studying them, and then doing your best to express your love in ways that fit their true needs and desires. This requires sensitivity, imagination, and creativity—trying to put yourself in the other person's place and figure out what is best for them.

The truth is that every person requires a different approach of love. What makes one person feel loved may leave another person cold. Showing love effectively means figuring out what says love to another person and taking the trouble to say "I love you" in a way that really communicates. It means knowing that David loves to sit outside at dusk with a glass of something cold or that Anissa loves movies—and doing my very best to make those things happen.

I might add that this process of studying the people we love and fitting our expressions of love to their needs is an ongoing one. People change, and their needs change—which means the expressions of our love will need to change accordingly.

I have a beloved friend who is going through a very difficult time in her life. She is trying to figure out who she is, what she's doing, and why she's doing what she's doing...and she's very distraught about the whole thing. Because this woman is my friend, I want to show love to her the best I can. For right now, I've decided that the best kind of love I can show her right now consists of nothing more than two good ears.

I've always enjoyed spending time with this woman. Our times together are delightful and inspiring. But these days, even after we have spent a couple of hours together—which we always do—I usually feel I have said nothing of any value. I haven't done anything that is tangible. I've just sat there and listened while she talked. And it helps! I can see it happening. As my friend talks and I listen, I can see the problems gradually shifting in her mind. The process of telling me her troubles helps her restructure them and get some insight on them.

So that's my love gift to my friend these days—just listening. Some years ago, though, when our children were small, my love gift for her was caring for her boys so she could have a little time for herself. And during another period my love gift to her was helping her decorate her house; we painted rooms together. (She gave me similar gifts of love, not to mention the splendid gift of her companionship.)

My point is that love manifests itself differently at different times and in different circumstances. This will be true of everyone you love—not only your friends, but your husband, your children, your parents. What helps your daughter feel loved at age two may be inappropriate at age 14. What feels like love to your husband in the early stages of your marriage may not have quite the same effect years later. The basics will probably remain the same, just as people's fundamental temperaments and the underlying reality of God's love remain constant. But if you want love to thrive in your home, you'll need to stay current of the love "sizes" of those you care about.

The next basic principle for creating a loving home atmosphere may sound a little strange at first, but I think it's one of the most important: *Organization helps love thrive.* This is a very practical reality. Organization is what ensures that your loving intentions actually get carried out in meaningful ways. Organization makes certain that birthdays are remembered, that cards are mailed, that gifts are wrapped and on time, that special celebrations get off the ground.

Remember the organizational tools I mentioned in an earlier chapter? Since I first created a home of my own, I've used those same tools—my notebook, a calendar, my systems for handling paper efficiently and storing little-used items—to organize my love for my family.

My notebook, for instance, includes a running list of birthdays, anniversaries, and other special days. I use it to remind me not only of when those days fall, but when I need to shop for cards and gifts and get these items in the mail. Along with the dates, I keep records of what I learn about people's preferences—colors, fragrances, sizes, interests—to help me buy appropriately.

My organized storage system allows me to buy gifts and wrapping supplies when the price is right or when I happen upon just the right present for a coming occasion. I put these items away in my marked boxes, write them down on index cards that tell me what box they're in, and then locate them quickly when the need arises. My paperwork handling system allows me to keep track of important information about people I care about—such as changed addresses or news about weddings or bereavements—and to stay current in my relationships through correspondence.

For the most important people in my life, I even keep individual file folders to hold correspondence, notes about milestones in their lives, special memories, gift ideas, and just thoughts about our relationship. I draw upon these files whenever I'm trying to think of creative ways to show love for these people. When my godson, Willard, enrolled in a religiously oriented prep school, for instance, I noted the fact in my notebook and Willard's folder and put in a reminder that he needed more theologically challenging books from me in the future. When my calendar told me Willard's birthday was coming up, my Willard file already contained several appropriate gift ideas.

Can love thrive in an unorganized household? Certainly. I've visited homes that were cluttered and inefficient and very loving. But I've also seen homes where disorganization led to disappointment and resentment—birthdays forgotten or thrown together at the last minute, clutter leading to irritation and fights, lost items and last-minute efforts depleting stores of goodwill.

Organization helps nurture a loving atmosphere by cutting down on that kind of stress—it helps keep my loving gestures from falling through the cracks. I find organization also enables me to carry through more effectively on loving intentions and great ideas. When Anissa married, for instance, I was able to empty three storage boxes and two shelves of family heirlooms I had set aside years ago for just that occasion, including a silver monogrammed teaspoon that had been passed down from Mabel and Eric, David's grandparents. Without my organized storage system, I feel sure I would have lost or forgotten half those items.

I would add that maintaining an organized household in itself can be a gift of love to your family. This is a reality many spouses and children would never express and, indeed, might not even be aware of. When you make the effort to be organized, you're really giving your family (and yourself) a gift of peace, serenity, reduced stress, and heightened efficiency. You're making space for your whole household to focus on dreams and goals and interests…and space for love to thrive.

Here's another basic principle that has helped me express my love to others effectively and maintain a loving atmosphere in my home: *Love thrives on a balance of spoken messages and acted-out messages.* Simply put, it's important to express your love through both words and deeds.

This may sound too basic even to point out. But most of us, I've observed, tend to feel more comfortable with one form of expression than the other. Some of us—often, but not always, women—thrive on giving and receiving verbal affirmations. We feel comfortable with language. We warm to words of love. Love feels more real to us, and less ambiguous, when it is spoken or written. And this is all well and good. God made us this way. And God, remember, spoke his own love to us from the beginning as the Word.

But spoken love is not the most comfortable or natural means of expressing love for everyone. Many people—often, but not always, men—prefer to express their love through actions. To them, acted-out love feels real and solid, while words can seem insubstantial. Mowing the grass, taking care of chores, building cabinets in the kitchen, earning a living, remaining faithful, expressing love through physical touch—all these are part of their preferred love language. And this means of expression, too, has its roots in the love of God. From the beginning, God gave his love to his people not only by what he said, but by what he did—creating us in the first place, saving Noah from the flood's destruction, giving descendents to Abraham, rescuing the Israelites from slavery, and so on throughout biblical history.

In Christ, of course, God gave us the living Word—the ultimate expression of love both spoken and acted out. In a sense, he also showed us what can happen when we combine both words and actions into shaping a loving home. No matter which form of expression is more comfortable to us, if we want love to really thrive in our homes, we must develop both. We must learn to speak—and to hear—the words *I love you*, verbally reassuring the people in our lives that we care. We must learn to write them down, in notes, letters, e-mails, and in lipstick on the bathroom mirror. And we must put those words into action as well, showing our love through acts of help and service and tangible gifts of love.

Here's another vital principle that has helped me express my love to my family and friends in ways that really communicate: I've learned that *love thinks both little and large*. I create a loving atmosphere in my home when I search for a variety of ways to express love to the people in my household.

In a sense, little daily gestures form the foundation of a loving home atmosphere. The goodbye kiss, the hello hug, a quick "I love you" phone call or a note in the briefcase, a little present "just because," a decision to speak gently instead of nagging or lecturing—any of these can keep a sense of love flowing in the home. Little gestures can be delightful surprises (a flower on the nightstand or in a Coca-Cola bottle tied with a big red bow—one of my all-time favorite gifts from David). They can be expressions of grace (a decision to overlook a slight or a mistake). They can simply be a part of a fabric of routine (a note about where I've gone and when I'll be home). Whatever form they take, their combined impact on our lives—and the atmosphere of love in a household—is far from small. The more I have become aware of their power, the more I have tried to work these little gestures into my days and closest relationships.

There are times, however, when love calls for more than a little gesture. Sometimes it's appropriate to pull out the stops and do something special, something that requires planning and attention. I'm a firm believer in family celebrations that affirm our love for each other in dramatic, highly memorable ways—like the retirement party where a group of young men David had mentored produced a hilarious skit about his past, present, and future or the prewedding surprise in which a big collection of Anissa's friends showed up wearing the ugliest bridesmaids' dresses they could find—big gestures that require an investment of both imagination and resources. They take up our time and call on our best organizational skills. But they are infinitely worth doing on a regular basis because of the message they convey: "You are worth all the trouble."

Such "big" expressions of love also support another important principle of shaping a loving atmosphere, which is that *love thrives on memory.* A loving home is held together by a fabric of memories—shared traditions, special days, and unforgettable moments. It's hard to underestimate the powerful connection between memories and love. In a sense, the greatest, most fitting love gift you can give the important people in your life is to be intentional about creating and preserving loving memories.

Making memories has always been a priority in our home, especially once Anissa was born. Because of my own rather barren background, I've been especially aware of how important it was to orchestrate memorable and fun moments—again, both big ones and little ones. When we toted our red "You Are Special" plate to restaurants and sent it to the kitchen to be filled (sometimes to Anissa's acute embarrassment), we created memories. When we threw one of our sometimes-corny theme parties, we created amazing memories. Even today, as we enjoy together the process of planning Anissa's wedding, we are aware of renewing our love by creating memories.

You can give your own family a gift of love not only by looking for ways to make memories, but also by working to *preserve* those memories. I don't mean that you need to spend hours a week pasting pictures and clippings into albums. Though scrapbooking can be a wonderful, fulfilling experience and a completed scrapbook can be a treasured love gift, there are many other ways to keep your home atmosphere warm by preserving memories. If you don't have time to put pictures into albums, you can keep them filed in boxes or send them to loved ones over the Internet. And be sure to talk about your shared memories as well. Children love to listen to stories about "when I was little," and writing out such memories can be a wonderful gift of love. In our house, we love to reminisce about special times we've enjoyed. We love to sing old songs and hymns that renew memories of special times we've spent with those we care about.

Family traditions are an important part of this make-a-memory mind-set, a way of creating new memories even as we preserve the old ones. Each time our family holds hands around the table and says grace over a meal, we are remembering past times together and creating new memories. When we trim the tree at Christmas with the faded paper chain Anissa made at age three or hold a lobster race on Christmas morning (prior to cooking the lobsters) or hide a gift for a "hot or cold" game of hide-and-seek or ask and answer an "Otto Dumb Question" at one of our holiday gatherings, we are building ties of memory and love.

Traditions can be as simple or elaborate, as old-fashioned or as quirky, as your family wants them to be. They can involve little acts of love—like the stuffed pooch our family used for years as an expression of love and encouragement. He would show up in the most unlikely places—in the dishwasher, the flower bed, the mailbox—as a gesture of love, a sign that someone had secretly taken care of a chore for someone else. They can also be tied to daily or seasonal routines—meals and holidays are natural places for traditions to develop.

One family I know of had a tradition of having extra "guests" show up in the family manger scene—a ceramic figurine, a tiny stuffed animal, even a Star Wars figurine or a parade of tiny plastic ants. Each would arrive secretly, stay briefly to "worship" and be admired, and then disappear—only to be replaced by another mysterious pilgrim. Guests got involved, too, bringing secret visitors to the manger when they stopped by to share holiday greetings. In the process, memories were made and warm past memories were renewed. Even in that slightly offbeat household, love thrived.

Here's an important principle of maintaining a loving household that you might not think about: *Love thrives when you help others show love to you.*

Even people who are uncomfortable with expressing their love enjoy that sense of having picked just the right present or said exactly the right thing or helped in a way that made a difference. When you help your husband or children do this for you, you are really giving them the gift of satisfaction and self-esteem.

How can you help others show love to you? At the most basic, it's a matter of self-awareness and simple communication. It involves understanding what sort of words and actions make you feel loved and then letting others know what those things are.

I don't mean that you hand out catalogs or buy your own gifts to make sure you get exactly what you want. But there's nothing wrong with giving clues and hints. There's nothing wrong with answering if someone asks you what you would like. There's nothing really wrong with saying something like, "I would love to have that book for my birthday."

Now you may think, "That's crass and selfish. How dare I dictate what I expect to receive?" But it's not really dictating. All these hints have nothing to do with being selfish and demanding. The point is to give your loved ones the joy of giving—without having to be mind readers.

There's nothing more gratifying, after all, than really *connecting* with a gift of love, expressing love in a way that hits home with the other person. With just a little bit of help and some hints, you can give your family and friends that gift of gratification.

If you want to do this, of course, you have to be honest with yourself and others about what kinds of love gifts really matter to you. Is your birthday important to you? Do you feel bereft if no one honors you on Mother's Day? Do practical presents such as tools or appliances leave you depressed or exhilarated? Does an expensive present thrill you or leave you fretting about damage to the family budget?

Once you figure out these things about yourself, you owe it to those who love you to spread the word—gently, of course, and not in the context of a recent disappointment. I would never suggest you turn up your nose at a love gift because it doesn't meet your specifications. Far from it. I'm simply suggesting that being honest and vulnerable about your own expectations can help shape the overall climate of love in your home.

There's another side to this issue of accepting love, and it's equally as important as making our love needs known. That other side is learning to receive love in whatever way it comes to us.

We all have times when we miss the target in expressing our love—when the sweater doesn't fit or the words fall flat or the favor is misinterpreted. And we all have times when love is handed to us in forms that we have a hard time appreciating. We may receive a blender or a vacuum for our birthday in place of the jewelry that would thrill us. Or our birthday card is corny or mushy when we prefer a little humor. Or our family's clumsy attempts to please us by cleaning the house actually leaves more work for us to do.

What do we do then? If we truly want to foster an atmosphere of love, we say thank you—and mean it! We remember that the act of kindness is what matters most.

A loving household thrives on giving and receiving, expressing and communicating, but no one will get it right every time. If we want to nurture the loving atmosphere in our homes, therefore, we must learn to see past the *expression* of love to appreciate the *intention* of love.

OTTO'S MOTTO

All gifts are acts of generosity.

I'm not talking about politeness here. I'm not talking about pretending to like a gift when we really hate it. I'm talking about an act of imagination and faith—learning to acknowledge and receive love in the spirit in which it is given. It's learning to look past the gift and love the giver…all in the context of God's overarching gifts of love.

This is precisely what I have had to do with my memories of growing up. I've had to look past how I felt to see the evidence that my parents were trying to love me. And while this hasn't erased the pain of the past, it has helped me move past the pain into forgiveness and even gratitude.

There's a reason that all of this can work, of course. It's the reason love is even possible for any of us, the reason we treasure gifts of love from one another, the reason it's possible to nurture an atmosphere of love in our homes.

Ultimately, we can only give one another the love that has been given to us.

The book of James puts it this way: "Every good thing given and every perfect gift is from above, coming down from the Father of lights, with whom there is no variation or shifting shadow" (1:17).

The love we give each other, the love that fills our hearts and shapes our homes and thrives on observation and organization and memory and honesty, is simply a reflection of the Father's dependable and astonishing love.

The kind of love that, no matter what our own failures, will never fail us.

A Moment of
REFLECTION

1. When you look back at your childhood home, do you think of it as a loving place?

2. Can you think of a time when lack of organization got in the way of expressing your love? Can you think of times when overorganization or obsessiveness hindered your loving expression? What do you think is the key to balance in this area?

3. Does the idea of helping others love you leave you a little uncomfortable? Why do you think that is true?

LOVE

$\mathcal{N}$othing is sweeter than love, nothing more courageous, nothing higher, nothing wider, nothing more pleasant, nothing fuller nor better in Heaven and earth, because love is born of God, and cannot rest but in God, above all created things. Love feels no burden, thinks nothing of trouble, attempts what is above its strength, pleads no excuse of improbability. . . Though weary, it is not tired; though pressed, it is not straitened; though alarmed, it is not confounded; but, as a lively flame and burning torch, it forces its way upwards and securely passes all.

THOMAS À KEMPIS

PART THREE

Making Your Home a Place of Growth

❦

Grow in the grace and knowledge of our Lord and Savior Jesus Christ. To Him be the glory, both now and to the day of eternity.

2 Peter 3:18

FIFTEEN

LIKE A WATERED GARDEN

IT'S NOT EASY TO STOP a living thing from growing.

Growth is built into the very cells of God's living creations. In almost any climate and almost any soil—even a desert—*something* will grow.

But it's clear to me every day as I drive around Phoenix, Arizona, where we live, that a desert is not the same as a garden. I happen to believe that a thorny bush or a soaring cactus can be beautiful, but a cactus patch is not the same as a blossoming flower bed or a fruitful vegetable garden.

Human beings, too, are programmed for growth. As long as minimum requirements for nutrition and protection are met, most children will manage to reach physical adulthood. But as you well know, a lot more is needed for a child or an adult to grow strong and wise and competent, to actually contribute to human society and bear fruit for the kingdom of God.

The question, in other words, is not really whether we grow.

The question is *how* we grow.

And that brings us back once more to the subject of home.

Your home, remember, is holy ground. And one reason it's holy is it's a place for God's people to grow. It provides fertile soil where you and your family can blossom into the people God had in mind when he first created you. That's what God intended when he created human beings with the potential to grow and to know him—and homes where that growth could be cultivated and nurtured. Is it an accident that the first human home was in a garden?

I love the passage in Jeremiah in which God promises, "I will be the God of all the families of Israel, and they shall be My people....and their life will be like a watered garden, and they will never languish again" (Jeremiah 31:1,12).

For someone who loves gardening and has learned how to do it in a hot, dry place, that's a vivid, beautiful picture of what can happen in the holy ground of home. Home is supposed to be a place where people not only manage to grow, but are nurtured, encouraged, and helped to grow into the mature, loving, and godly people God created them to be. It's a place of rich resources and careful tending, where lives are shaped to produce fruit for God's kingdom.

Who grows in such a garden? Everybody!

Quite obviously, home is a place for children to grow and flourish. It's where those rosy little baby toes learn to walk and run, to fit into booties and then sneakers and finally pumps. It's where they learn to say "please" and "thank you," to brush and floss, to ask God for help, apologize when they've wronged someone, and forgive someone who has wronged them. It's also where they have the best chance of getting to know and love Jesus.

But growth has never been just for children. Human beings, perhaps alone among God's creation, are made to continue growing our entire lives. I don't mean we are supposed to get physically bigger—though many of us do! But the Bible makes it clear that we are to continue growing toward full emotional, spiritual, and physical maturity, a process that takes a lifetime and more. The apostle Paul described this process eloquently in Colossians 1:9-12:

> For this reason also, since the day we heard of it, we have
> not ceased to pray for you and to ask that you may be
> filled with the knowledge of His will in all spiritual

wisdom and understanding, so that you will walk in a
manner worthy of the Lord, to please Him in all respects,
bearing fruit in every good work and increasing in the
knowledge of God; strengthened with all power,
according to His glorious might, for the attaining of all
steadfastness and patience, joyously giving thanks to the
Father, who has qualified us to share in the inheritance of
the saints in Light.

Home is supposed to be a growing place for parents as well as
children. It's a place where men, women, and children can find the
safety to try new things, the grace to learn from our mistakes, the
space to be creative, the discipline to order our lives, the courage to
reach out and help others grow. No matter what your circumstances, your home can be a beautiful and fruitful watered garden.

Watered gardens just don't spring up complete in the desert,
however, and a home that fosters mature growth doesn't just
happen either.

A garden requires a plan—a vision for what the desired outcome will be—and preparation—the beds marked and bordered,
the soil enriched and irrigated. The seeds, once planted, must be
carefully and attentively cultivated using a variety of gardening
techniques, and the growing plants must be protected from weeds
and harmful insects.

And here's the interesting thing: In the holy ground of your
home, you are called to be both a gardener and a garden. The basic
design and the ability to grow is purely God's gift to you. He is the
one who made us all with the urge to grow, who can be trusted to
care for us as we stretch our tender leaves toward the Son. But *how*
we grow and how we help others in our household grow are also
parts of our sacred responsibility as homemakers and homekeepers.

As parents, especially, but also as men and women growing
toward full maturity, we are called to catch a vision of growth for
our homes. We are called to do the work of maintaining our lives
as watered gardens—cultivating the holy ground of our home so

that it remains a growing place, equipping all of us to bear beautiful fruit for the kingdom of God.

A Moment of
REFLECTION

1. What does it mean in practical terms for your home to be a growing place?

2. Can you think of aspects of your home that actually hold you back from growing? What can you do about that?

3. How can working to make your home a haven of peace help it be a place where people grow?

THE GOD OF GROWING THINGS

You visit the earth and cause it to overflow;

 You greatly enrich it;

 The stream of God is full of water;

 You prepare their grain, for thus You prepare the earth.

You water its furrows abundantly,

 You settle its ridges,

 You soften it with showers,

 You bless its growth.

You have crowned the year with Your bounty,

 And Your paths drip with fatness.

The pastures of the wilderness drip,

 And the hills gird themselves with rejoicing.

The meadows are clothed with flocks

 And the valleys are covered with grain;

 They shout for joy, yes, they sing.

PSALM 65:9-13

SIXTEEN

WHAT ARE YOU PLANNING TO GROW?

IF YOU WANT TO MAKE YOUR HOME a growing place, you have to start by looking ahead.

Good gardeners do this. They don't just start out one morning with a hoe and a packet of seeds picked up at random from a shelf. Instead, they start out with a vision for what the mature garden will be like. They may spend long winter months browsing through seed catalogs and gardening books. They may sketch layouts or plans, send off soil samples for analysis, or research gardening techniques. They certainly must assess the time they have available, the money they can spend, the possibilities of the particular site they have chosen, and the requirements of their particular climate. Where I live, in hot, arid Arizona, it means learning that tomatoes must be planted in January, corn can only be planted in August, watering is a constant requirement, and while some items will never make it in the heat of southern Arizona, others will thrive.

Most important, gardeners must start with a clear understanding of what they are trying to grow. Not just whether they want to raise vegetables, flowers, herbs, or cactus—but whether they prefer to cultivate roses or raise pumpkins or sink pots of mint in the soil or combine barrel cactus with saguaro. All other preparations will depend on the basic consideration of what the crop will be.

In the garden of your home, especially if you are raising children, your vision of the finished project makes all the difference—and finding such a vision really is the heart of finding your purpose as a mom. Daily decisions become easier if you keep in mind what you are trying to accomplish, what kind of human being you hope your home will produce. This basic picture will help you choose your battles, decide your strategies, and focus your parenting efforts on what is truly effective. During those awkward stages when nobody seems happy and nothing you do seems to make any difference, that vision of your child or yourself as a blossoming, fruitful adult—and your faith that your vision can become a reality—may well be all that keeps you going.

Fortunately, the Bible actually gives us a clear idea of how God wants us all to grow. The stories of the Old and New Testaments paint us pictures of imperfect people who nevertheless keep moving forward in obedience (Abraham, Sarah, Moses, Joseph, David, Mary, Peter). The wisdom books (Job, Psalms, Proverbs, Ecclesiastes, Song of Solomon) are packed with advice about becoming a wise, mature, productive person. Prophets such as Isaiah and Jeremiah and Ezekiel are quick to spell out what kinds of behavior pleases God (faithfulness, repentance, care of the poor), what makes him angry (worship of other gods, corruption, materialism), and how God helps his people grow (through chastening, encouragement, hopeful promises, and practical help). Paul's Epistles and the other letters in the New Testament not only dwell on what real maturity means and give us vivid pictures of successful growth (see 1 Corinthians 13 and Galatians 5); they are also full of very practical advice about how we can grow in ways that please God (see especially 1 and 2 Timothy and the entire book of James). And of course the Gospels give us the powerful picture of how God incarnate grew: "Jesus kept increasing in wisdom and stature, and in favor with God and men" (Luke 2:52).

Studying God's Word, then, is a wonderful way to catch a vision of what you want your garden to grow. It's your most important handbook throughout the growing season—which includes not only those crucial years when your children are home, but your whole life. But it's still up to you to work out the specifics, to figure out how God's gardening instructions apply in the holy ground of your own particular home.

I urge you to be especially intentional and specific about your vision for your children's future. When your children are fully grown and ready to bloom, what will they be like? What will they know? What skills will they have? What will they desire, and what will they love? Will they be a source of encouragement or discouragement to those around them? What will they be able to accomplish for the Lord?

I did exactly that when my Anissa was just three or four. I sat down and made a list of what she should know at certain ages—by age ten, twelve, sixteen, upon leaving home, and so forth. At the time I was very task-oriented, so my list was mostly concerned with practical abilities. I wanted her to be able to keep her personal space clean, to cook, have good manners, care for younger children, wash and mend clothes, and so on. By the time Anissa was in her teens, in fact, the items on my list were more or less checked off and I had almost forgotten the list. But I realized just how important such intentionality had been when our 15-year-old daughter was preparing to leave for a summer in France. A friend of mine, who also had a 15-year-old, asked me, "Aren't you concerned about how she'll behave, how she'll take care of her possessions?" I realized then that such a concern hadn't crossed my mind. Of course Anissa knew how to behave. I'd taken care of that years ago because I took the time to look ahead to what we wanted to accomplish.

Such visions of future fruit make a big difference in the decisions you make now—what you do to influence your children, to nurture and encourage them, to discipline and shape them. Remember the picture on the front of the puzzle box? The picture on the front of a seed packet works the same way. It helps you keep your finished product in mind when all you can see at the moment is a plot of dirt, a tangle of weeds, and a whole lot of work to be done.

It's in the midst of those day-to-day chores, after all, that discouragement sets in most quickly and progress tends to slow. It's easier to stay in bed for another hour instead of hitting the pavement for a morning walk or hitting your knees for prayer. It's simpler to let your children watch another hour of TV than thinking of something creative for them to do or insisting they finish their chores. It's easier for you all to sleep in on Sunday morning than go through the hassle of getting the family to church. Without the vision of where you're going, the path of least resistance often seems the logical choice. But when you have a clear sense of what you're working for, the hard choices become easier and the work becomes a joy.

There's no reason, by the way, to keep your vision of growth a secret from your children. They can benefit from knowing what you desire for them, what you believe is important, what you are trying to achieve in your parenting. Chances are, they'll find this knowledge helpful in making decisions and charting their growth. (It always helps to be given a roadmap for where you are trying to go.) And the very fact that you care enough to make a plan is clear evidence of your love for them.

So what objectives will you aim for in raising your child? What characteristics do you hope he or she will have as an adult? What kind of person will the holy ground of your home produce? I'd like to suggest some basics—a list of qualities and achievements for a young person who is ready to blossom and bear fruit in the world.

1. *I want my garden to grow a man or woman who has said (or is ready to say) the Big Yes to Jesus.* Working toward this objective, I believe, is a parent's most important responsibility. You have been given the gift of helping a little sinner—and all babies, even the most adorable, are born sinners—become a saint. You are called to the ministry of evangelism in your own home, to create an environment in which a child will learn about the God who created

him, who loves him with everlasting love, who has redeemed him through his Son, and who wants to live in relationship to him. You are called to witness to your children, to influence them gently to choose the path of Christ, to show them through your words and your example what it means to follow Christ. You are called to help your children develop a capacity for faith, trust, and obedience, to prepare them for God's transforming work in their lives. How do you do all this? Here are some ideas:

- You can model authentic discipleship by showing your children what it's like to live as children of the King.

- You can give them a taste of heaven by treating them the same way your heavenly Father treats you—with firmness, consistency, kindness, correction, and gentle guidance.

- You can teach children in age-appropriate ways about the realities of sin, redemption, and their need for salvation.

- You can prepare them for obedience by training them to obey and respond to authority.

- You can tell them Bible stories and help them memorize Scripture.

- You can take them to church for worship, fellowship, and teaching—but remember that you are their most important teacher.

- You can supply them with Christian books, tapes, and other resources.

- You can expose them to loving Christian mentors and role models.

- You can share your own reasons for following Christ and some of your personal experiences.

Above all, you can pray both for them and with them. Pray specifically for their safety, their growth, and their salvation. You might even want to use pen and paper to help you remember all the things you want to talk to God about where your children are concerned. In 1989 I did just that. I actually wrote out a four-page prayer for Anissa that I've been praying most days for her ever since. I keep that handwritten sheet of paper with me in my prayer closet to remind me of how I want to pray for my daughter—the issues that I need to discuss with God on a regular basis. For instance, I want to always pray that "she would make choices that would not have severe and long-lasting consequences." (I've made a new one for her and her husband.)

None of this guarantees that your children will grow up to be believers. No one can say the Big Yes for anyone else. But by showing your children what it means to follow Christ, teaching them about what God requires, and training them to live in ways that make following him seem more natural, you make the Big Yes easier.

In the next few pages, I want to get a little more specific and suggest some desirable growth outcomes for children in your home—some objectives to keep in mind as you work to make your home a growing place. But keep in mind that I'm talking vision, not goals. I am speaking of what you hope to grow, not what you intend to achieve. The distinction is important if you want to avoid frustration.

A goal is measurable and achievable, something you can acquire by your own efforts. And the simple truth is that a parent can't force a child to achieve what the parent desires. As a parent, you do have significant influence—perhaps more than you'd like. But you still can't force a child to grow up a certain way. A child's own choices will play a part in the person he becomes. So will his inherited temperament and gifts and constitutional weaknesses. Outside influences and events will contribute—as anyone who grew up in wartime, a depression, or a poor neighborhood will attest to.

It is entirely possible, in other words, for a parent to do everything right and raise a child who turns out all wrong. Free will and choice belong to each of us. It is also possible—and I believe this happens a lot—a for a parent to make mistake after mistake and still produce a splendid young adult. In parenting, as in gardening, it's important to be faithful, but the outcome is ultimately in God's hands.

I don't know about you, but I find that a big relief. Helping children grow while we're still trying to become more mature ourselves is a daunting responsibility. We can take a lot of the pressure off by remembering that both we and our precious sons and daughters are children of our heavenly Father, who loves us. We are an important part of God's plans for us and our children, but he can do a lot without us—or in spite of us. We and our children are safe in his hands. The more we trust in him, the closer we follow him, the more fruitful our lives will be.

2. *I want my garden to grow a "faith literate" man or woman.* This means someone who knows the Word and who understands the faith. Home should be the first seminary and the best theology class a child will ever have.

At the very least, I believe, a child who leaves your nest should know the books of the Bible and the order in which they appear. He should know God's plan of salvation—humanity's sinful nature and need of God, God's gift of Christ, man's need to put God first—and the major themes of the Bible. He should be able to recite or at least paraphrase the Ten Commandments, the Twenty-third Psalm, the Sermon on the Mount, the Lord's Prayer, the Golden Rule, and the Great Commission, as well as key prayers, responses, or creeds in your particular church community.

An arsenal of memorized Scripture and a collection of hymns and songs will provide invaluable spiritual sustenance. (Choose your favorites and sing them often with your children.) A basic understanding of biblical and church history—how the Bible came to be, how the major denominations differ, and so on—can also be very helpful, and stories of "faith heroes" can help this information come alive. And I believe a child should also know why you have chosen to be a part of a particular community of faith.

3. *I want my garden to grow a man or woman of prayer.* Your modeling makes a big impression in this area. As children see you read the Bible daily and pray—and live as obediently as possible— they develop a basic understanding that this is what people do. Prayer, meditation, journaling, fasting, giving, and other spiritual disciplines don't seem strange or foreign to a child who has seen it on a daily basis and seen its effectiveness in the life of her mother.

Involving children in your daily disciplines is also important. Family devotions and mealtime blessings are part of the training process. So is reading Scripture with them, praying with them on a regular basis, and helping them become aware of how God works in the world.

At our house, for instance, we used to play a form of "I Spy" in which we took turns saying, "I spied God doing something today." Then we would share an observation of something we observed that only God could do—anything from making the wind blow to helping Anissa remember to say her prayers.

Helping children memorize certain prayers can be an effective way of teaching them how to pray. Setting aside quiet times for reflection in the course of your day helps children become more comfortable with silence and to learn to listen for God's still, small voice. Involving children in decisions regarding your family's tithe of money and time helps them learn the dynamics of stewardship. You may even choose to fast as a family, learning together the meaning of depriving yourself for spiritual purposes.

4. *I want my garden to grow a self-disciplined, restrained man or woman.* Deferring gratification, setting aside self-will, and making present choices in the interests of future benefit are learned skills. You help children learn these skills by training them from an early age to control their impulses and subjugate their will. This means that you must discipline yourself not to give in to their every whim. At the same time, you give children choices whenever you can. You keep in mind that your goal is not to force children to do things your way, but to instill in them the ability to delay gratification and

work toward worthwhile long-term goals. Training your child in time management, study skills, habits of organization and maintenance, courtesy, and obedience to authority are all part of helping her grow to be self-disciplined and self-controlled.

5. *I want my garden to grow a person of character and integrity.* This means someone with the strength and courage to act and speak honestly, to stand up for his beliefs, and to work hard. You do this, once again, by example and by training. Children will learn from your example of integrity, but they must also be guided to do the right thing even when they would prefer not to.

6. *I want my garden to grow an appropriately educated person.* There are simply some things that a person living in the world needs to know—and childhood is the best time to acquire a lot of that information. I am often amazed at children's ability to take in and retain information. Whatever they learn as a child will probably be with them the rest of their life. It's really worth the effort, therefore, to fill their memory banks with information and understanding that will equip them to live in the world and give them a solid foundation for future growth.

What are the vital elements in an appropriate education? Certainly, a child should know how to read and write, how to do basic calculations and higher math, how to locate a place on a map. He needs a solid grounding in literature, science, and social studies and the study skills to further his own education. To progress in our society, a child needs some pieces of paper—a high-school diploma or the equivalent and either technical training or a college degree.

Growing appropriately educated children means arranging for your children to acquire the academic knowledge and skills necessary. You can do this by teaching children directly, arranging for experts to teach children as they grow older (and monitoring the influence of these experts), supplying children with resources to learn on their own, and training them in basic self-discipline and work habits as well as specific study skills. It also means studying your children and doing what you can to tailor each child's learning to his or her particular skills and interests, providing each child with an education that not only prepares him for life in general, but also lays a foundation for a meaningful career.

Keep in mind that a particular child's needs may change as he or she grows, so you'll need to keep adjusting your education plans. One child may thrive in public school year after year, another child may do best in a private school or homeschool setting; another child may need to change schools several times. Remember that even when you choose for others to teach your children, you are still the one who is responsible for their education.

7. *I want my garden to grow a person with practical skills.* In addition to an appropriate academic education, every child, male or female, needs to learn at least the basics of caring for themselves and others. As I mentioned earlier, when Anissa was small, I actually made a list of skills I wanted her to master before she left home, and I made sure we had worked through the list before she left for college. I encourage you to make up a similar list when your children are small. Yours may not be exactly the same as mine, but it will give you something to shoot for as you teach your children how to be responsible members of society.

Here is a list of some of the basic skills I believe every child should master before leaving home:

- Cooking—how to prepare at least two or three simple meals (and clean up afterward)

- Clothing care—sorting clothes, using a washer and dryer, ironing, folding, basic clothing repair (either sewing or use of iron-on tape)

- Housekeeping—how to make a bed, vacuum or sweep, clean a bathroom

- Hygiene—dental care, nutrition, exercise, and cleanliness

- Home repair—how to use a hammer, screwdriver, wrench, and pliers

- Auto—how to drive and maintain a car

- Finance—how to draw up a budget and manage a checkbook, how to avoid credit card debt

- Employment—how to apply for a job, dress for an interview, and be a dependable employee

8. *I want my garden to grow a culturally discerning person.* From the time that Jesus was here on earth, believers have lived in tension with the community around them. On the night before he left the earth, Jesus said specifically that his followers were "in the world" (John 17:11) but not "of the world" (John 17:14). He also taught that those who believed in him were to be salt and light to the world around them (Matthew 5:13-14).

Part of helping a child grow successfully in your home, then, will be helping them negotiate this "in but not of," "salt and light" position. They need to learn to engage the surrounding culture enough to have a voice but also to develop the strength and discernment to cope with cultural pressures—materialism, violence, inappropriate sexuality, rampant addictions, and ungodly ideas.

All this can be tricky. It's hard to know when you should insulate your child from worldly influences (TV, movies, games, friends) and when you should help them learn to engage the world. For most of us, this is a learn-as-you-go process. In general, I believe, it's best to start by protecting children and then gradually moving them toward experiencing the dominant culture with your input and guidance. What limits you set will depend on your own beliefs and your reading of your child. I urge you to give thought to this issue from an early age and develop a plan for helping your child learn to live as salt and light in a culture that desperately needs a godly influence—remembering always that we can trust God to protect both us and our children and to redeem even our mistakes and bad choices.

9. *I want my garden to grow a person with self-understanding.* Psalm 51:6 says, "Behold, You desire truth in the innermost being,

and in the hidden part You will make me know wisdom." That means that God, who knows everything about me, wants *me* to know everything about me. He wants his followers to know themselves—and helping children know themselves is an important part of a parent's responsibility.

OTTO'S MOTTO

Light the Light—don't curse the darkness.

Every child offers a unique blend of talent and temperament, ability and disability. Each child's history, however short, has shaped his thinking and personality. Each child who comes to Christ is spiritually gifted for the benefit of the body of Christ. It is your job as a parent to help your children discover all these special attributes and learn to use them in positive ways.

You can do this by studying your child, pondering on who she is (as Mary "pondered" the events of Jesus' birth in her heart), and adjusting your methods of encouragement and discipline to fit the specific child. You can suggest activities that require your child to use her abilities and develop her gifts. You can also help her learn about herself by pointing out abilities you see in her and making it clear you expect her to do the best she can with these abilities.

Helping children understand themselves also means helping them appreciate the special privileges and responsibilities of being male or female. Teach your sons and daughters to celebrate their masculinity or femininity and to relate to the opposite sex with courtesy and respect.

10. *I want my garden to grow a person who can live with others.* This means someone who has developed relationship skills, who understands courtesy and etiquette, who has learned to communicate clearly, who understands how to give and take, and who will eventually be able to handle a committed relationship. These

"people skills" are important subjects for teaching and training because they help children be successful in the world. Henry Ford once said he'd pay any salary to any man who could get along with people.

But being able to live with others requires something deeper than the ability to get ahead by developing people skills. It also means knowing how to love and give one's self to others, to understand forgiveness, and to handle conflict. Most of all, it means learning how to reach beyond "me."

Every baby comes into this world as a sinner, remember, and the essence of that sin is that every beautiful, adorable infant is inherently selfish. A baby's world is centered on "me"—feed me, hold me, burp me, change my diaper.

That's not the baby's fault, of course. It's just part of being born human. But growing to true maturity means learning to grow beyond "me" and learning how to reach out to others. It's learning to put God first and to consider others more important than self. It's learning to look at a hurting world and reach out to help, to know the joy of helping others. This final objective, of course, brings us back full circle. Because selfishness is sin, and the only dependable remedy for sin is Jesus Christ, we come back to the reality that the first priority for any home garden is raising children who are prepared to say—or already have said—the Big Yes to the Lord.

Meeting these ten basic objectives is just the starting point, of course. What I've just given is the picture of someone who is ready to embark on a productive life, not someone who has finished growing. And it goes without saying that these ten growth objectives are not just for children. They are essential to anyone's healthy development, fit goals (but not final ones) for any Christian believer. And they are certainly hallmarks of growth for parents as well as children. Even as we prepare our children to say yes to God; teach them Scripture; show them how to pray; help them develop self-discipline, honesty, and integrity; stretch their minds with learning; teach them practical skills; help them learn to understand their culture and themselves and to relate better to others, we must be growing in these areas as well.

What happens after your children leave home? Your home can still be a growth center for yourself, for those who share your space, and for those you welcome into your home. At the same time, your children will be establishing their own homes on holy ground, using what they have learned in your home to transform their own walls and roofs and floors into living, productive, growing places.

And God the Gardener, who made us to grow and who loves all growing things, will surely say, "That's good!"

A Moment of REFLECTION

1. If you have children at home, can you picture them grown and ready to launch out on their own? What do you imagine they'll be like?

2. Which of the ten items on my list are most important to you personally? Which strike you as the most difficult or challenging? Do you have any to add to the list?

ARE YOU GROWING LIKE JESUS?

One of the main purposes of Jesus' coming to earth was to show us how to live. . .and how to grow. Luke 2:52 tells us that "Jesus kept increasing in wisdom and stature, and in favor with God and men." What a wonderful model for us to follow both in our own growth and in raising children.

- ⊛ *Wisdom—gaining in knowledge, understanding, and discernment; developing a sense of right and wrong; understanding when to stand firm and when to bend.*

- ⊛ *Stature—growing to physical adulthood, but also becoming a person of integrity, character, and strength.*

- ⊛ *Favor with God—growing into someone who loves and trusts God, who knows the Lord's voice and obeys, who delights in God's Word, who loves God and others and puts that love into action.*

- ⊛ *Favor with Man—growing into someone who gets along with others as much as possible without endangering his relationship with God. A person who is kind, courteous, thoughtful, loving, who puts others first, who gets along without mindlessly conforming.*

SEVENTEEN

CULTIVATING YOUR INFLUENCE

SHE WAS A CITY GIRL WHOSE PARENTS didn't garden. The only gardening tools she ever saw in their garage were a lawn mower and an edger, and her parents frequently hired a lawn service to take care of even those basic chores. But my friend loved plants, and she loved spending time in her friends' gardens, so she finally decided that gardening was a hobby she'd like to explore.

She started by reading articles and books. She learned about growth zones and soil acidity. She discussed her project with gardening friends and garnered a wealth of tips and hints. She even experimented with starting a compost heap. But then, when the time came to actually break the soil and start the garden, she found herself stuck.

She explained her problem to me succinctly: "I have all this information, and I know what I want to do in this garden, but I still don't have any idea what to do with a hoe!"

The truth is, tools make an important difference in a garden. Every dedicated gardener I know loves her tools—the shovels and rakes and wheelbarrows that help her turn a bare plot of ground into a blooming paradise. (I will not let anyone use my hand clippers. I even hide them from David.) And every successful gardener must learn how to use these vital tools to most effectively cultivate growth—turning soil, chopping out weeds, spreading compost and mulch.

And yes, I believe you also need tools and techniques to make your home a growing place, to help your children grow up the way you envisioned, the way God expects, the way that best fulfills their potential and brings them the best satisfaction. What are the most important cultivation tools a parent can use? That answer could fill eight parenting books, but I would like to suggest four of the most crucial:

- modeling
- teaching
- training
- grace

My editor tells me that her constant advice to writers of novels is "show, don't tell." That's valuable advice for raising children too—and it's the essence of what I mean by *modeling*. Yes, there will be times when you have to tell children what to do or even force them to do it. (That's where the other tools come in.) But what you show children in your own life—your attitudes, your habits, your reactions, your commitments—often makes a far deeper impression.

It's almost impossible to underestimate the importance of modeling healthy attitudes and good character for children honestly and authentically. From the time they are very small, they watch us carefully. They copy our good habits, our bad ones—even the way we walk and sneeze and laugh. They internalize powerful lessons about what is possible, what is right, how to act, and how to view the world from the way we treat them, the way we treat others, the way we respond to God.

What are some things you can help your children learn by your example? On the simplest level, they learn how to do things—walk, talk, pick up toys. They learn how to work hard and get things done, and they also learn there are times to rest in the Lord. They learn to get on their knees to pray or to lift their arms in praise.

On a deeper level, when you show children love, they learn what real love looks and feels like. When you show up to pick them up as promised, they learn to trust God for their needs. When you act cheerful in the midst of a bad day, they learn that their joy need not be dependent on circumstances. When you talk out a conflict with a friend, they learn how to give and take in relationship.

Truth, especially, is something that children learn best from their parents' example. Are you always truthful with your children? Do you mean what you say and say what you mean? Do you keep your promises to them? If you tell them lunch will be ready in a minute, lunch should be there soon. If you say you'll come and tie a shoe, you should be there. If you promise certain consequences for their actions, you must follow through. This kind of truthfulness from parent to child not only teaches the child to be truthful in her own life, it also builds a very strong foundation for a child's trust in the truthfulness of our heavenly Father.

Faith is another vital characteristic to model for your children. When children see you persevering in your commitments and trusting God to take care of you and your family, they come to understand the power of hanging on. When they see you working through your problems, they will be less likely to give up when they encounter problems of their own. When they see you relying on God to help you and care for you, they learn to have faith as well—and in this area, especially, your example has a far more powerful impact than your words ever will. I can still see Anissa, after yet another lecture from me—I did far too much lecturing in those days—rolling her eyes and saying, "Oh, great—more victorious Christian living!" She'd had quite enough of the words. But her life was shaped by the *example* of victorious Christian living she saw in our lives and those of other adult role models.

Gratitude is yet another quality that children must see in your example. Your children should see that you look with grateful appreciation and admiration to your Maker for the many gifts you have been given—including them. Let your children know that you are grateful to God for them. And let them see the power of a grateful spirit in shaping a joyful, productive life.

There is almost no limit to the things you can teach children through your example. You can model a love of books and a taste for learning. You can model an open mind and a willingness to forgive. You also model good habits, such as prayer, cleaning up after yourself, keeping your closet organized, even flossing. Most important, you model love. You express your love to them with words of encouragement and affection. You show them what love looks like by the way you treat them and the way you treat others.

By itself your example will not guarantee that your children will "catch" what you want them to. But your example shows them what is possible. It demonstrates what matters enough to invest your life in. By staying married to your husband and working out your problems, you demonstrate that people really can honor commitments for a lifetime—a powerful and life-giving message in this day of disposable marriages. By praying about your problems in front of the children—and sharing with them the answers to your prayers—you demonstrate that prayer is an important part of life. So much of what your children become, they will pick up by watching you every day.

And make no mistake—children notice what you do. They copy what they see, and children can be remarkably accurate. Unfortunately, what they copy from us is not always what we intended.

Have you ever had one of those awful moments when you realize your child is acting exactly the way you do at your worst— making excuses for a task undone, stuffing himself with junk food, telling a little white lie to avoid a hassle? If you haven't, you probably will. I can still see our little Anissa shaking her finger and raising her voice to her dolls in an eerily accurate imitation of one of my lectures. The sad truth is that children don't copy what you want them to see, but what they *really* see. And children seem especially quick to pick up on our negative examples and copy them.

This reminds us, of course, of how important it is for parents to keep on growing, pressing on toward what God wants for us. A good example is not something that can be faked. We must strive toward fruitful maturity not only for our sakes, but the sakes of little ones who may be watching and copying us. This is both a matter of our own integrity and of love for our children.

If we want our children to grow up to live organized and peaceful lives, in other words, we must learn to be organized and peaceful ourselves. An unruly mother cannot expect her children to be anything other than unruly. If we want our children to grow up loving and giving, we must learn to reach out to others and put their needs ahead of our own. If we want our children to grow up to be self-disciplined and self-controlled (or lively and imaginative, or hardworking and dedicated), we must work to cultivate those qualities in our own lives. My dad's favorite adage—"Don't do as I do; do as I say"—simply doesn't work.

At the same time, we might as well face the fact that none of us will ever be able to present a perfect example to our children. The sad truth is that we are all sinners. Our children are sinners too. And while they are perfectly capable of coming up with sinful behavior and attitudes of their own, they're going to watch us and pick up on our shortcomings as well. The "sins of the fathers" are passed along to children not only through our DNA (in the form of original sin) but also through our example.

The good news is this very reality gives us an opportunity to point children toward the remedy for sin, Jesus Christ. We do this by being honest with our children about both our shortcomings and our aspirations. We do it by letting them see us confess our sin to God and accept his forgiveness. We do it by showing we can trust God to cover our failures and help us all grow.

The most important thing you can model for your children is the process of coming to Jesus for help, forgiveness, guidance, and the grace to handle whatever life throws at you. If you model for your children nothing more than persistent faith in God, you will have given them what they need most.

Example is one of the most powerful—and challenging—tools you have to help your children grow into what God wants them to be. But example alone, as we have seen, is not enough. For one thing, no parent is perfect—and most of us want children to learn good habits we may not have perfected.

In addition, children can be unpredictable in the lessons they learn from a parent's example. They watch us carefully, but they don't always interpret our behavior or our motivations the way we would like them to. They may misunderstand, or they may simply not want to "hear" the message. When you model unselfishness by letting a child have the biggest piece of pie, for example, the child *may* learn to be unselfish. But that child may also get the message that she deserves the biggest piece and should always get it.

In addition to setting an example for your children, therefore, you also have the responsibility to both *teach* and *train* them. These two techniques are not synonymous, although many people confuse them.

Teaching, essentially, means imparting information or demonstrating skills—giving facts, demonstrating techniques, explaining why. You can teach a child the multiplication table, the names of the stars or animals, the books of the Bible, the words and the meaning of John 3:16. You can teach him the secret of making a bed with hospital corners or the right way to chop an onion. You can tell him stories, teach him songs, show him what the notes mean on the piano. You can explain why it's important to treat other people with kindness or wash the dishes after every meal or to settle disagreements before going to bed. You can teach the reasons why you think it's important to act a certain way. With a little research and a little homework, you can even teach something you didn't know before—and learn right alongside the person you are teaching.

OTTO'S MOTTO

It's hard to teach what you don't live.

Teaching can take many different forms, as the words of Deuteronomy 6:6-19 implies:

> These words, which I am commanding you today, shall be on your heart. You shall teach them diligently to your sons and shall talk of them when you sit in your house and when you walk by the way and when you lie down and when you rise up. You shall bind them as a sign on your hand and they shall be as frontals on your forehead. You shall write them on the doorposts of your house and on your gates.

Look at all the teaching tools that one verse recommends—lecturing, repetition, class discussion, visual aids, even incorporating movement into the lesson to reach children who learn better when they are doing something physical. You can teach a child by telling a story. You can demonstrate a skill and help a child learn it by doing. You can buy books, take the family to the library, invest in video instruction. You can make up memory games or have puppets act out what you want the child to learn. You can even have the child practice a new skill and teach by making comments along the way.

As I said earlier, one of my most useful teaching tools over the years with my daughter, with the women I have mentored, and with the women I teach in the Homemakers by Choice organization has been my Otto's Mottos—brief, memorable, and repeatable statements. And boy, do I repeat them, because I have found that repetition can be a valuable teaching tool.

Because different people process information in different ways, effective teaching will never be a one-size-fits-all proposition. Some people learn best visually—through pictures, charts, and diagrams. Others learn best by hearing—through repeated instructions. Still others incorporate information best kinesthetically, which means that they acquire information most effectively by moving and doing. Most children, I have found learn best through a combination of approaches.

For me as a parent and teacher, this tells me that my best teaching will be flexible and geared to the child's learning and temperament style. It also tells me that I need to pay attention and figure out how the child learns best. If I notice that a child tends to forget my words quickly, for instance, I might try other ways of getting the same message across. Instead of just telling her how to make a bed, for instance, I might show her how I make a bed or even find a children's book with pictures of a bed being made. Even better, I might involve her with tucking the corners and smoothing the sheets, helping her to learn by doing.

At the same time I am teaching this child how to make a bed, however, I will also be in the process of training her to make her bed on a regular basis. And here we come to the fundamental difference between teaching a child and training him. While teaching involves putting information into her head, training involves shaping her will and her habits. When you consistently require a certain behavior—daily study, making the bed, answering a neighbor politely—and you enforce that behavior until it becomes automatic, you are training the child. Training is an intentional effort to affect a child's overall interaction with you and the world.

At its most basic, training is necessary to children's physical safety and well-being. That is why you must begin training a child long before you begin teaching him and before he is old enough to copy your example. You can train an infant to fall asleep in your arms or in his crib, to prefer a particular (washable!) blanket or toy, to eat at certain intervals. As he grows a little bigger, his life may actually depend on your training him to obey your voice and a few simple commands. Long before a toddler can understand the physics of a one-ton truck encountering a 25-pound body, he can be trained to hear the word "no" and respond to it.

As children grow, good training is essential to instilling in them the kinds of habits and attitudes that will help them in the future. Self-discipline, self-control, good mental, spiritual, and physical habits, can all be accomplished by training. So can attitudes of gratitude and contentment.

In order to effectively train a child, it's important to understand from the outset what training is *not*. Training is not the same thing as *breaking* the will or the spirit of a child. It's not a matter of changing a child's basic temperament and personality—nor of giving in to that basic nature. And it's certainly not the same thing as imposing your own will by simply forcing the child to act as you see fit.

This is something I learned from hard experience, because my mother essentially parented me by imposing her will on me. From the time I was tiny, she told me what to do and I obeyed. She was a strict disciplinarian, and I was a very disciplined little child. But my mother never really understood how to train me in *self-discipline*. As a result, the minute I got out from under my mother's influence, I did exactly what I wanted to do. She had raised me to do 13 loads of laundry a week, to keep a house spotless and absolutely tidy, to wash the top of the refrigerator every day.

Even worse, when Anissa came along, I reverted to my mother's habit of imposing my will on her. I was very strict with Anissa, very determined that she was going to do things my way. After all, that was what I learned from my mother. (To be fair, my own personality might have something to do with it as well.) Fortunately, the Lord and some precious friends helped me understand a little better the line between shaping the will and forcing the will, and I became a better mother as I went along.

If training is not breaking the will or imposing someone else's will, what is it? It's a slow, patient process of expectation, correction, repetition, and practice. Training requires a lot of patience, a lot of perseverance. It works best with a soft voice, a gentle spirit, and a view of the required outcome.

Think of a gardener training a tree to grow along a fence. If he allowed the limbs to grow and then forced them in position, they would probably snap. Instead, the gardener checks the young tree every day, pruning off shoots in the wrong direction, and gradually and gently bending the remaining limbs into position. By the time the tree is grown, it has taken the shape the gardener planned all along.

It is true that training often involves some form of coercion or discipline. It often means pushing children to do what they don't want to do or depriving them of something they desire. But the *purpose* of training is not to punish or coerce, but to help children develop habits and attitudes that will help them in the future.

What are some of the areas in which you can train children? Here are some possibilities:

- practice good hygiene
- be appropriately responsible for themselves
- work cheerfully, energetically, and efficiently
- do chores "first and fast"
- organize their possessions and make decisions about what goes and comes
- be content and defer gratification
- go the second mile and bear one another's burdens
- persevere with a task until it is completed
- put others ahead of themselves
- talk politely to adults

The list could go on and on. I very consciously trained my daughter to practice gratitude, for instance, by repeatedly asking her to "give me ten." I would have her hold up her hands and actually count off ten things she was grateful for.

One young woman told me her mother always trained her children to come out and help her unload groceries whenever she pulled into the garage and honked! And there's nothing really wrong with training your children in ways that make your life a little easier. But once again, the real purpose of training children is to help them grow into responsible, unselfish, competent people.

These three techniques—modeling, teaching, and training— are different but not mutually exclusive. You can do all three at the same time; in fact, you're *supposed* to. One method of helping a child grow will support and complete the other.

A very simple example is helping a child learn to brush her teeth. You model an example by making sure your child knows that you brush *your* teeth. You teach a child *how* to brush her teeth—how to hold the brush, how to put on toothpaste, how to brush up and down. At the same time, you train the child to brush regularly first by brushing her teeth for her, later by taking her to the bathroom, putting the toothbrush in her hand, and standing by while she brushes. Later you may reinforce this lesson on tooth brushing with a chore chart, checking teeth to be sure they are clean, and perhaps waking up a child who forgot and making sure she goes ahead and brushes.

Or say, for example, that you want to help your elementary-age son to learn what to do when he's done something wrong. You want him to accept responsibility for what he's done, to confess his wrongdoing to God and to the person he's wronged, to apologize and ask forgiveness, and also to handle any residual guilt feelings. Obviously, such a lesson will be learned over time and the specifics will depend on both his maturity level and the nature of his wrongdoing, but here are some of the ways you can use your example, your teaching, and your training to help him grow in this area.

First, you give your son a powerful example when you actually apologize to him for a mistake you've made—perhaps losing your temper and yelling at him for a small infraction. You also teach him something important by letting him hear you confess your sins to God—this must be an honest confession, not a "show" to teach your son a lesson.

At the same time, you can teach your son about how repentance and forgiveness work through a number of methods. You could read him the parable of the unforgiving servant in the Bible. You can explain to him *why* you chose to apologize to him or someone else and why he should learn to do the same—because God tells us to, because it's a way to live at peace with others, because we usually feel better. You may even teach him words to use when he needs to pray to God for forgiveness.

In the meantime, you help him internalize this important truth by insisting that he do the right thing. If you catch him hitting his sister or stealing candy from the corner store, you insist that he apologize and, if possible, make amends. If necessary, you go with him and stand next to him until he does it. If his apology is ungracious, you may stand there until he does it right.

How you mix the three techniques will depend on many factors—the age of the child, his particular temperament and personality (some children need more persuasion than others), even your own level of maturity in certain areas. I find that many parents struggle in the area of example and that others find it tricky to balance teaching and training. Some are more comfortable explaining things than with making sure a child does what he needs to do. Others feel comfortable insisting a child act a certain way but don't really know how to teach.

All this is just another reason why we must focus on our own growth even as we help our children grow. If you're like me, you'll find that nothing grows you up as quickly—or throws you on the Lord's mercy as readily—as raising a child.

Modeling, teaching, training—all are important tools for helping children grow. You need all three, working in combination, to help your garden grow well. But you need another tool, and you need to use it often.

That fourth tool is grace.

Even as we work to teach our children and train them and model right behavior to them, we need to be in the constant process of extending *grace* to them. Giving grace is a matter of being patient with the growing process. It's a matter of allowing for mistakes and encouraging second tries. It's a matter of focusing on the possibilities of a relationship and the potential of a yet-imperfect person, expecting the best and forgiving the worst, and helping those we love find new solutions when none of the old ones have worked.

When our Anissa was growing up, she knew that if she didn't make her bed in the morning there was a very good chance she would hear over the public-address system at school that her mother wanted her to come home and do it. She knew for certain that her father and I would follow up on any of our requirements and make sure she followed through as well. At the same time, she knew that on certain, random days her mom would go through the house shouting "grace day, grace day"—and that meant she was excused from all her chores for the day. In this way, we were able to model God's grace while remaining firm about our expectations.

The most important thing to recognize about this final teaching tool is that it's for every growing thing, not just the children in a family. Grace is God's overwhelming gift to all of us—imperfect children and imperfect mothers and imperfect single people as well. So many young mothers I meet with are very hard on themselves. They have high expectations for themselves and their families. They are acutely aware of the mistakes they make and are worried about making more. (I'll have to admit that at times I've been that way too.) Without big doses of grace, they risk overloading on stress and responsibility.

The good news is that God has offered us grace in abundance—remember, "grace on grace on grace." The even better news is that God is the loving heavenly Father of both us and our children, and our future is ultimately in his hands, not ours. Children are not our possessions. They are not extensions of us. They belong to Jesus.

Yes, there is a lot we can do to help our garden grow. Yes, we have enormous influence on our children, even the possibility of doing damage. But God covers it. He really does. I am deeply humbled as I look back on my own parenting fiascos and realize what a wonderful job God has done with our Anissa both through us and in spite of us.

And when I think of it, God uses those same four tools to help all of us grow in wisdom and stature and favor with God and man:

- He *models* right living for us through the example of his Son and the story of his dealings with humankind from the beginning.

- He *teaches* us through his Word and through the witness of godly people.

- He *trains* us through circumstances and the conviction of the Holy Spirit.

- Best of all, he gives us *grace* to learn from our mistakes and try again.

With God as our Gardener, how can we do anything but grow?

A Moment of REFLECTION

1. In your family of origin, what are some positive and negative things you learned from your parents' example? What are some of the things you believe your children are learning from watching you?

2. Most parents prefer to help their children grow either by teaching or by training. What is your tendency?

3. What are some of the challenges you have faced in raising children or helping others grow? In helping yourself grow?

4. Do you think it is possible to give too much grace to your children? What is the difference between indulging them and giving grace?

TEACHING AND TRAINING

*D*o you know the difference? Here's a quick outline of the differences:

- 🕭 *Teaching involves knowing. Training involves doing.*

- 🕭 *Teaching gives information. Training gives skill and practice.*

- 🕭 *Teaching fills the mind. Training shapes the habit.*

- 🕭 *Teaching gives the child what he does not have. Training enables a child to make use of what he has.*

- 🕭 *We teach words. We train children to speak.*

- 🕭 *We teach a biblical truth. But we train a child to find the truth for himself and make it part of his life.*

EIGHTEEN

HOW DOES YOUR GARDEN GROW...BEST?

Mary, Mary, quite contrary," goes the nursery rhyme, "how does your garden grow?"

For parents and gardeners alike, the more important question is "How does your garden grow...best?"

With or without you, your child is going to grow. But what can you do to encourage that growth and help everyone in your household reach their full potential? What is the best way to help your garden grow lush and green? Here are some ideas:

One of the most basic things you can do is spend a lot of time with your children—because *a garden grows best when you are present.* Homes, like gardens, need frequent and watchful tending if they are to produce optimal crops. That means that your garden will yield the best fruit if you're at home as much as possible.

This applies especially if you have children at home. Your children need you to be *physically* present with them as many hours as possible, especially in their earliest years. They need you to be *mentally* and *emotionally* present as well—watching them, studying them, thinking about them, interacting directly with them without a wandering mind or a heart that yearns to be elsewhere or feelings of divided loyalty. Missionary Jim Elliot, whose widow,

Elisabeth, has been an important mentor in my life, once put it this way: "Wherever you are, be all there."

I am not really talking here about the issue of whether a mother should stay home with children or work outside the home. That's an issue for another book. (Mine is called *The Stay-at-Home Mom.*) But whatever your choice and your circumstances, I would urge you to be honest with yourself about how much time you spend with your children and how involved with them you are when you are together. During times of stress or seasons of pressure, it's too easy to let yourself become distracted, to just go through the motions of parenting—and that's true for stay-at-home moms as well as those who work outside the home. A stay-at-home mom can be a mall mom, a TV mom, or a Bible study mom. Staying at home with your children does not make you fully engaged.

While God, who knows our sorrows, will often cover for those times when we neglect to pay attention to our children and our own growth, we can always help our children grow by choosing, on a moment-by-moment basis, to be fully present with them during the hours we are together and being sure they are closely tended when we must be away.

No matter how you choose to be present to your children, I urge you to remember as well that *a garden grows best when it is well ordered.* I don't mean rigid conformity or neatnik sterility. I mean, essentially, a house where:

- It's possible to find the scissors, and you don't have to run to the store every time a child needs a compass for math class.

- Meals happen at predictable intervals—and at predictable places, especially the dinner table.

- Bedtimes, wake-up times, and nap times occur at more or less the same time each day—and happen the same way (perhaps with a story at night).

- Family rituals are lovingly planned for and kept up.

"But the children don't mind if we eat dinner on trays in the living room because I didn't have time to clean off the table." That may actually be true. Many children do seem to enjoy chaos, and they're experts at creating it. But in the long run, children need a certain amount of order to thrive. And because they are just beginning to learn how to create order for themselves, they need you to order their garden for them.

How many times have you sighed because your little son or daughter wanted to hear the same bedtime story or watch the same video for the hundredth time in a row? Children love (and need) repetition and predictability far more than adults do. In a world where everything is new, they appreciate being able to know how their own small world operates. They like knowing when they can expect bedtimes and mealtimes to happen. They love to hear the story of their birth and flip through their baby books, and they treasure even the silliest family rituals—even, secretly, after they grow into impossibly "cool" adolescents. And although they may deny it energetically, they feel more secure in a household with rules and expectations, as long as they are also taught *how* to follow the rules and meet your expectations.

An obvious benefit of an orderly household is that it helps children learn to be organized themselves. From your example, your teaching, and your training, they learn how to create order and develop the self-discipline to make it happen.

My experience is that relationships also tend to improve in an orderly household. Clear expectations and predictable discipline cuts down on nagging and screaming matches. Regular mealtimes enhance family togetherness. Children who understand *how* to please you are more likely to *try* to please you. And the simple fact that stress is lower in an orderly home—no more panicked rushes to clean the house or get ready for an appointment—freeing everybody to put their energies into learning and growing.

How do you keep your garden orderly? The organization strategies listed in part two of this book can help. A few additional considerations can help you tailor your organization plans to the purposes of growth:

- Pay special attention to organizing children's living space so that they can keep it neat themselves. Everything should be within their reach, bed linens should be easy for them to handle, and every toy should have a home.

- In addition to your daybook and calendar, consider keeping a family calendar in a central place so that everyone knows what's coming.

- Assign chores on a regular basis rather than just as they occur to you. Use chore charts, job jars, or other gimmicks as needed to make sure children know what is expected of them.

- Make sure your children understand how to do what is expected of them. Show them, watch them, correct them.

- Resist the urge to involve your children in every sport, every musical opportunity, every extracurricular activity. Choose a few—the ones that you believe will mean the most in the long run—and dare to eliminate the rest.

- Enhance family togetherness by having regular meals together—even if it's only one or two sit-down meals a week. Schedule them and make them happen.

- Make a point—occasionally—of throwing the rules out the window! Stay up late together to watch a movie. Serve ice cream for dinner—the whole dinner. Blow your entire daily schedule on a trip to the zoo.

This last point is important, because it is certainly possible for a house to be *too* orderly, to be organized yet barren. I grew up in such a home. My mother was highly disciplined and organized almost to the point of fanaticism, in spite of the fact—or perhaps because of the fact—her emotional life was often out of control.

The bookshelves in our apartment were empty of books; the mantelpiece was a bare stretch of wood. We cleaned the top of the refrigerator every day and washed the curtains weekly. My life with her consisted mostly of school and chores and, when I grew older, an after-school job.

Thankfully, I turned out all right—mostly because of God's grace, but also because of some special people in my life who understood that *a garden grows best in rich soil.* These were people like my Aunt Pat, who taught me hospitality, and a woman I worked for named Mrs. Ruble, who shared with me her lively love of beauty. People in my church introduced me to the wealth of Scripture and the warmth of Christian family and fellowship. School friends took me home with them and shared their own rich family lives with me. My father provided me with satisfying work experiences. I was fortunate to grow up in a city that offered museums and art galleries that fed the spirit of a little girl growing up in a largely unimproved patch of soil.

I'm not trying to criticize my mother here. She loved me, and she did the best she could to raise me. My point is that God has created a rich and beautiful world for us to live in, and I believe he wants the holy ground of our homes to be just as bountiful. A growing place is one that is rich in resources—books, pens, paper, art supplies. It is rich in relationships—men, women, and children doing things together and enjoying each other's company. It is rich in experience and practice—cooking together, hiking together, learning new things together, doing chores together, serving God together. And it's rich in beauty—music, art, growing things.

If you want your home to be a growing place, I encourage you to be intentional about providing a rich environment for growing. Decorate your home with beautiful and uplifting objects. Stock the den with musical instruments and learn to make music together. Throw a family party. Read books to each other while you clean the kitchen. Lie outside on a blanket and try to learn the names of the stars. Serve together at a food pantry, a soup kitchen, or a church cleanup day. Create scrapbooks. Take the family to concerts or plays in the park—a perfect venue for introducing wiggly children to culture. Establish traditions such as always reading the Declaration of Independence or the preamble to the Constitution on the Fourth of July. And by all means, plant an actual garden!

Remember always that "rich" doesn't have to mean "expensive." In fact, it's easy to fall into the trap of substituting consumerism for enrichment. Playing music together or making Christmas cards at the kitchen table is a far richer experience for children than holing up in separate rooms with headphones and computer games. Your creativity, your determination, and your own appreciation of God's wonderful world are what enrich the soil of your growing place. The more you use them now, the fewer regrets you'll have in the future.

A garden needs more than rich soil, of course. So here's another important principle to keep in mind: *A garden grows best when it is watered.* Those of us who dwell in arid Arizona are acutely aware of this reality. Without water, the richest soil produces stunted crops or nothing at all.

How do you water the soil of your home garden? First, by liberal doses of encouragement and praise. Children absolutely thrive on praise—but it has to be honest praise. Don't fall into the trap of enthusiastically applauding every little movement just to help children "feel better about themselves." I assure you, they can tell the difference between empty flattery and true praise.

If you want to help your children grow, get in the habit of noticing, applauding, and encouraging their significant efforts and real accomplishments. Be specific about what you like and admire. Don't stop with "good job," but also add "I appreciate the fact that you remembered to make your bed this week." When Anissa was little, we literally applauded her efforts—giving her a big hand when she made a good effort. And Anissa, who will always be a bit of a ham, responded to our honest praise with her best efforts.

One of the most effective ways to water your garden is to respect and celebrate each child's uniqueness. Treasure and respect the specific qualities that make individual children different and special, including:

- *Their feelings.* They don't have to dictate behavior, but they are real. Never belittle a child's feelings. Instead, acknowledge honest emotions and then try to help the child handle them.

- *Their individuality.* Don't expect your children to be just like you...or anyone else. Instead of trying to make them in your image, help them find out who they are meant to be.

- *Their opinions.* All children, even the tiniest, have a point of view. You don't have to agree or give in, but you need to listen and acknowledge that children have the right to their opinions.

- *Their abilities to think and to solve problems.* Maintaining authority doesn't mean ignoring your children's good sense!

I'll never forget driving in the car with Anissa one day and hearing her say, "No, Mommy, that's not the way you turn." Now, this was quite a few years ago when Anissa was in elementary school. I was insulted when she told me that. I thought, *Don't tell me what to do. You're just a little kid. I'm the driver and the mother. I'm the one in charge here.* And then, of course, I went ahead and turned the way I had planned—which was the wrong way. What I was just beginning to learn back then was that my daughter watched carefully and she remembered everything. When it came to issues of who-said-what or what-happened-when or which-way-do-we-go, she was usually right. She still is. Over the years, I've come to rely on her accuracy and appreciate it instead of getting huffy. In the process, we both have grown.

One of the most specific instructions the New Testament gives about parenting is found in Colossians 3:21. In this verse parents (fathers, specifically), are instructed not to "exasperate" their children. When we respect our little ones, we'll find it a lot easier to train them effectively, to encourage them and help them grow instead of provoking and frustrating them.

And while you're at it, make sure your children know you are praying for them to grow, for prayer is the other essential way to water your garden. The more prayer you pour out on the holy ground of your home, the more growth you can expect. Actually, I suppose, what you're praying for is rain. After all, it is God who does the actual watering in your garden. But the act of prayer makes a big difference because it keeps you in touch with the Gardener.

Don't forget that *a garden grows best when it is protected.* A watchful gardener is on the constant lookout for invaders that could harm his crops. He sprays for bugs. He picks off caterpillars. He sets up scarecrows to discourage hungry birds. He may surround the whole place with a fence to prevent people from trampling the crops. He may even have to shield the garden from too much of a good thing—shading tender seedlings from the noon sun, for instance, or digging ditches to divert floods.

Protection is part of your job as a parent too. The world can be a dangerous place, full of physical hazards as well as people, ideas, and images that can stunt your children's emotional growth. Cars drive too fast through suburban neighborhoods. Choking hazards roll around on the floor. Fast food is both inviting and unhealthy. Pornography lurks on the computer. Doubt, cynicism, and disrespect are part of the public forum. And Satan is out there, too, waiting to tempt and devour us all.

But please don't panic as you read all this! Yes, the danger of the world is real, but Christ has overcome the world (see John 16:33). The Bible makes it clear that the Lord is a dependable, safe refuge. His protection for all of us is sure.

In addition, I think we need to keep perspective. The media is fond of warning us about everything that can go wrong with our children, but by far the majority of young people manage to grow up healthy and happy. And while it's natural to want to protect those we love, it's also possible to stunt their growth by becoming overly protective.

How do we keep a balance? First, by focusing on trust, remembering, as the old prayer goes, that "only in thee can we live in safety." And second, by matching our protection with the developmental needs of children.

Babies and toddlers need close supervision and safe places where they can play without fear of injury. Young children need to be shielded from ideas and images they aren't ready to handle—including, all too often, the daily news. But as children grow, protection becomes less a matter of keeping them safe and more a matter of preparing them to live in the world. They need to know what's out there and how to handle it. And they learn this best with the guidance of a loving parent.

Exactly how you go about doing all this will depend on your own interpretation of where danger lies and your understanding of what God expects of you. But here are a few basic ideas:

- Establish and enforce rules to protect children from physical, emotional, and spiritual danger. First train them to follow the rules. Later, as they grow, you can teach them by explaining your reasoning—and gradually change the rules.

- Watch what they are watching—television, movies, video games. Pay attention to underlying ideas and assumptions as well as language or "niceness."

- Don't necessarily depend on ratings to decide whether a movie or television show is all right for your children to watch. Do your homework. Read reviews and descriptions of actual content. (Internet sites such as www.screenit.com are very helpful for this.) If in doubt, watch a movie yourself before you allow your child to see it.

- Whenever possible, watch or read questionable material along with your child. Comment on what you see and relate the material to what you believe in as a family.

- Know your children's friends well. Invite them to your house and observe them interacting. Keep a close eye on your child's ability to be "salt and light" without being unduly influenced.

- Protect children from their own greed and laziness. Don't give them everything they want.

- Teach your child some basic street smarts—how to defuse a fight, what to do if confronted by a bully, and so on. Small or timid children may well benefit from a self-defense class.

- Don't terrify your children with too much emphasis on "what can happen." Make it clear that you and the Lord are in charge of keeping them safe. Their job is to learn and grow.

Are you already feeling tired from all the work this kind of gardening entails? Are you beginning to wonder if you'll ever succeed as a gardener? If so, please stop to consider another essential ingredient for helping your garden flourish: *Your garden grows best when you have some help!*

While you and your husband bear the primary responsibility for helping your children grow, you are not the only human influence in their lives—and you're not supposed to be. As they grow older, especially, you will share some of your influence with others: grandparents and other family members, friends, teachers, coaches, and mentors. This is both appropriate and necessary. Your children need to be involved with godly men and women who will love, pray for, teach, and counsel them. One of your responsibilities as a parent, in fact, is to consciously connect your children with older people who can help them grow in positive ways. In the teenage years, especially, young people benefit from the loving influence of adults who aren't their parents.

A friend of mine, a gentle soul who tends to be soft-spoken and "reasonable" in disciplining her daughter, loves to tell how much she appreciates her daughter's godmother, who grew up in a tough neighborhood and got in a fair amount of trouble before coming to Christ. When the time came to talk to little Elizabeth about drugs, the two of them took very different approaches. Even today, Elizabeth likes to say, "My mom says that drugs aren't good for me and she hopes I'll be smart enough to stay away. Audrey says if I ever do drugs she'll kill me." It's a bit of a joke between the two of them, but the combined influence of mother and godmother made a big impression on a little girl.

Our Anissa, too, benefited greatly from the love and wisdom of older women in her life. From the time she was small, I consciously cultivated her relationship with older adults whom she liked and I trusted, women who were different from me but had the same belief system. (I have tried to play this role myself in the lives of other young people.) These mentors have often been able to talk to her when I couldn't and influence her in ways I never could—not to mention praying for her, caring for her, helping me see her more clearly, and correcting her when necessary. How often have I breathed a prayer of thanksgiving for these people who cared enough to love my daughter along with David and me. They have been so important in helping my own little garden grow.

When Anissa was preparing to be married, she personally honored these women with a "Women of Influence" brunch. Anissa did all the planning and most of the preparation herself. Fifteen women were invited. Fifteen came. And Anissa presented each woman with a written statement of gratitude and a tangible object that represented what that woman had contributed to her life. One woman received a telescope, for the gift of insight and vision. Another received a tiny knitted "blankie," representing comfort. I received a tool belt. And Anissa's mother-in-law-to-be received a disposable camera, still in its package, with the explanation: "You hold my man's history, the pictures of his past that you can share with me. This history is still in its package because we are still new to each other, but I look forward to learning about my husband from you."

Needless to say, tears were shed around that beautifully set brunch table. The gift of loving and godly influence for our children is a significant one.

Here's another contributor to optimal growth that you might not have thought of: *Your garden grows best when you let it be a source of joy.*

There's a reason that gardening is a hobby for many people. Yes, it's hard work. Yes, it can be frustrating. But gardening is also intended to be fulfilling and even fun. Most gardeners I know find a deep pleasure in the whole process—digging in the rich brown earth, searching out the first tender shoots, admiring the growing stalks and leaves, picking the flowers and harvesting the fruit. Even the hard work of tilling, weeding, and watering brings a certain satisfaction.

I believe God intends that same joy for all of us in our growing places. Your home, after all, is a gift from God, not a penal colony—and your children are supposed to be blessings, not burdens. Your garden will grow best when you not only love your children and help them, but rejoice in the whole process. Open your heart to the joy of watching people grow in your home. Take pleasure in your milestones, and be sure to celebrate the whole process of growing to maturity.

An old woman told me her goal when she was a young mother was to *desire* to be with her children all of the time. She knew she could not always be with them—and that such a constant presence might not be healthy. But the *desire* to be with her children, the ability to enjoy being with them, provided an important attitude correction. In this culture, parents often desire to pawn off their children as much as they can. Mothers long for freedom, for personal time. In the process, we often forget that our children are supposed to be a blessing.

If you are really struggling with this idea, if raising your children is a constant drain on your spirit, I would suggest you examine your life as a whole. It could be that you are overcommitted, trying to do too much. Are your priorities skewed? Are you trying to do everything by yourself, with no help or support? Are you neglecting your own growth and developing a martyr's complex?

I'll never forget a time when my David and I went out to dinner and he handed me a yellow legal sheet of paper, folded four ways. I carefully unfolded the paper and saw four words: I NEED MORE FUN.

That message hit me like a kick to the stomach. What could my husband possibly mean? Surely he wasn't saying I was no fun to live with. I've always been a fun person. Everyone else thought I was fun.

David didn't really explain; he just asked me to think it over. Over the next few days, as I prayed over those four little words, I started to understand what the problem was. I may have been a fun person, but I was also a very busy one. My work in ministry was growing and I was involved in a number of activities. I was having fun with everyone else but not at home. And I was taking care of my home, of course, but only in the sense that I kept things spinning. Everything was clean, everything was scheduled, but there just wasn't any excess energy for fun. Without meaning to, I had neglected to enjoy my wonderful husband and daughter, and all of us felt the absence of that rejoicing.

I'm not saying that everything in life has to be fun. I'm certainly not suggesting that it's your fault if you're less than happy with your life at the moment. I know that some mothers face pressures I cannot even imagine. But I also believe there's a reason the Bible urges us to "rejoice in the Lord always" (Philippians 4:4). We are called to rejoice not because circumstances are ideal—they rarely are—but because God is always at work to redeem us and draw us closer to him and bring about his kingdom. Even when we can't see any progress, God is at work in our lives. We can rejoice because God has promised to take care of us. And we rejoice because he has gifted us with so much—including the opportunity to grow and watch our loved ones grow.

So if you're finding it hard to locate even a little bit of rejoicing, that's something to ponder and pray about. You may discover that you, too, need some fun in your life. Or maybe a habit of complaining or negative talk is dragging you down. A young woman I know who is raising a severely handicapped child finds that she rejoices more easily when she resists complaining. Maybe you, too, need to stop complaining and trust God for what he is growing in your garden.

In the end, remember, we are all just assistant gardeners. Our heavenly Father is the one in charge of making things grow, and our involvement in the process is really for our own benefit, our own growth. So even as we do the work of tilling and watering and weeding, we need to relax and remember that God is still in charge. As Jesus told the crowds on the mountains—men and women, perhaps, who were overburdened with their own gardening chores—we need to "consider the lilies, how they grow: they neither toil nor spin; but I tell you, not even Solomon in all his glory clothed himself like one of these" (Luke 12:27).

A Moment of REFLECTION

1. In your own experience, what specific strategies have you found useful for helping your children grow?

2. What are some ways your growth was nurtured in your family of origin? Can you think of anything that slowed or stunted your growth?

3. Is anything currently hindering you from rejoicing in your garden and having fun?

Your Home Can Be a Growing Place

- ❧ Set up children to succeed by matching your expectations to their age and abilities. There's nothing wrong with high expectations, but make room for a learning curve.

- ❧ Focus on attitudes as well as actions, heart as well as hands.

- ❧ Set aside time and space for formal learning and study. When children are little, it can be a small table and chairs. As they grow they need a desk.

- ❧ Within your budget, enrich the learning environment of your home with books, games, and computers. But don't get caught in the high-tech money trap. There's plenty to learn the old-fashioned (and less expensive) ways.

- ❧ Plan activities that teach—a garden, a nature walk, a trip to a petting zoo.

- ❧ Encourage children to bring home items of interest to share.

- ❧ Encourage your children to invite friends over.

- ❧ Set aside structured times—mealtime is ideal—to converse and interact.

- ☙ *Monitor progress carefully and reinforce lessons. But remember that children often take in more than you think. Be willing to wait for results.*

- ☙ *Involve other trusted adults as role models, mentors, observers, and teachers of your children.*

- ☙ *Include interesting and diverse people at your table.*

❧

NINETEEN

GROWING IN YOUR OWN GARDEN

How long has it been since you thought about who you want to be when you grow up?

It's not really optional, you know.

No matter where you are in your life, even in the midst of your busy child-rearing years, you are still called to grow...and keep on growing. Physical adulthood is just the beginning of a lifelong process of growing into the person God has in mind for you to be.

But making growth a priority is not always easy. Sometimes just surviving seems to take everything you've got. When you're knee-deep in diapers or working late at night to pay the bills or worrying about your aging parents or trying to sell your house, "personal growth" may sound like an unachievable luxury or even a selfish indulgence. You may even feel quite satisfied with where you are in life and not feel the need to change anything.

But I know you. Even if we've never met, I know you.

I know you are a woman made in God's image. You are someone who has said yes to him and are doing your best to follow where he leads. And that means that somewhere in you—deep inside or right there on the surface—is a hunger to grow. You really do want to be more than you are. You want to experience more of what God has for you now, in the midst of your present life, and in the future.

God wants that for you too. The God of growing things has no intention of letting you stay where you are. He wants you to stretch, to learn new things, to live expectantly, to become more fruitful and productive, to keep on growing in your own garden, and to make that growth a priority in your life. (Remember, it's one of those things that nobody but you can do!)

How do you do that? Well, it's always a good idea to look ahead to the finished product—to consider what you want to grow into.

Have you ever stopped to envision what kind of old person you want to be? How you want to be remembered by others? It's an interesting exercise that can tell you a lot about yourself and help you make important choices now.

Do you want to be remembered as a person of wisdom, a person of energy and vigor, a person who accomplished something for the Lord? Do you see yourself as a happy grandmother baking cookies with your grandchildren? Do you envision yourself as a gray-haired lady who wears bright colors and takes college courses…a weathered but wise woman who sips tea with her younger sisters and advises them…a gorgeous, well-kept woman who inspires others with her energy? Do you see yourself enjoying the free time of your retirement by deep-sea diving—or diving deep into the Scriptures right there at home?

The first step in becoming this "fully grown" you of the future is envisioning the person you would love to be. Then ask, "Is this the person God is leading me to be?" and "Is this the person I am likely to become if I continue on my present path?" When you start asking these questions, the path to healthy growth almost always becomes a little clearer.

Obviously, this kind of looking ahead won't help much if you're not honest with yourself. If you are 45 years old and 75 pounds overweight, your objective of being a thin and vigorous 80-year-old will require you to make some significant changes or change your future vision. If you feel strongly that God is nudging you to sell your possessions and live with the poor, a dream of retiring to an expensive gated community may be out of the question.

But that's exactly the point. People can change, and people can grow, but a realistic examination of where you are and where you would like to be provides both a guide and a motivation for growth.

A friend of mine—I'll call her Dorothy—told me recently, "I'd give anything to look like Maria." Now Maria (not her real name) is one of those women who spends an inordinate amount of time and money on grooming. Her hair is always immaculately cut and colored and arranged. Her nail polish is never chipped. She moisturizes and exfoliates and waxes and tones—and she does look great. Dorothy, on the other hand, typically gives her hair and makeup a lick and a promise before running out to do what she likes to do. And that's fine. Dorothy is creative and industrious and gifted and makes an important contribution to the world. But when she said she'd give anything to look like Maria, I had to tell her, "No, you wouldn't." Dorothy has the same amount of time and money that Maria does, but she has made other choices about how to use that time and money—and she actually prefers the choices she has made.

From the time I was quite a young woman, I have seen myself as a gray-haired teacher who derives energy and pleasure from helping younger women learn to manage their lives. My friends laughed at me and raised their eyebrows because I thought a lot about being old. But my vision of a lively and useful old age has shaped my decisions along the way, helped me form goals, and brought me motivation as I worked to grow into the older woman I wanted to be. Today, I am happily living out the "senior dream" I've always had for my life.

Once you've got a future you in mind, consider how the basic cultivating tools of growth—modeling, teaching, training, and grace—can help you grow in body, mind, and spirit. How can you find the examples, the teaching, and the training you need to move closer to the person God had in mind when he created you? How can you fully avail yourself of the grace to grow?

When it comes to role models, it's always helpful to look back and consider where you came from. You may find that the example of those who raised you may give you fresh inspiration. Maybe you came from a family of strong, opinionated women, and remembering that strength can give you the courage you need to make a hard decision. But looking back at your childhood role models may also point out the need for replacing faulty models and changing some negative behaviors you learned in childhood. (We'll look at this in the next chapter.)

Quality teaching for positive growth is really not hard to obtain, although it may require some careful discernment. Books and magazines, courses and seminars can all supply quality instruction. So can Bible study groups and individual mentors. If your vision of a future you involves a career change or a completely new direction, you may actually need to go back to school.

As far as training is concerned, this is usually a matter for you and God. Other people can help in certain areas. A few sessions with a nutritional coach or a personal trainer can help you develop new physical disciplines. A sharing group may provide support and encouragement and accountability as you try to develop self-discipline in certain areas. But even with this support, training yourself in new habits requires perseverance and a daily reliance on God's strength.

Significant change is always a challenge, and the older we get, the harder it is to learn new habits and new patterns of behavior. (That's one reason it's so important to start early with children.) Most people find that training and retraining is a two-steps-forward, one-step-back proposition. Failures are likely. But you can help your growth significantly if you learn to "fail forward," relying on God's grace to redeem your failure and help you learn. Get in the habit of asking, "What can I learn from this?"

It helps to keep in mind that if we ask God to help us grow, he is faithful to do just that—and he may do it in ways we don't expect. The Bible makes it clear that God's ways are not our ways, and also that God actively disciplines his children for their own benefit. What this means to me is that growing in the Lord is partly a matter of keeping alert to what he might be doing through our circumstances.

Most of us find, in fact, that we do our best growing in times of difficulty, loss, and conflict. We humans are a stubborn lot who often require pain or significant discomfort in order to get serious about growing and changing. And God, I've learned, can be trusted to give us what we need—even if that means kicking us out of our comfortable nests or stripping our lives of things we truly care about in order to clear the way for new growth.

If you are going through one of those times when positive change seems to elude you, when you feel restless or confused, or when you don't like where you are but don't know where to go next, I would advise you to be especially watchful. Do your best to persevere in doing what you know to do, and open your heart to what God is preparing for you. In the meantime, you might want to consider ways you can set up your home and your life for optimum growth. Ask yourself the following questions, which are based on the principles outlined in the previous chapter.

Do I need to pay closer attention to my life? It's possible that you've fallen in the habit of ignoring certain issues in your life or distracting yourself from even seeing them. Remember Jim Elliot's words, when you're there, be all there. Are you all there for your own life? Are you paying attention to where you've been, where you're going, where you are in the present moment?

Can I organize or reorganize my household to help me move forward or meet new challenges? Perhaps you could rearrange your schedule to make space for a weekend retreat or clear out your spare room to make space for a sewing project.

Is my life in need of enrichment? Perhaps a new book, a new hobby, a new project, or a new friend is what you need to jump-start a new period of growth in your life. It helps to be intentional about surrounding yourself with people and objects that inspire you, uplift you, and help you learn.

Is my garden well watered? I am convinced that many adults become stuck in their own growth because they neglect their own "irrigation system" of prayer and devotion. The quickest way for your growth to wither is to get out of the habit of daily and deliberate communion with God.

It's important to note here that the water in your life won't always be on the surface. Many believers experience times when they are persisting in everything they know to do and nothing seems to be happening. Sometimes that means water is flowing underground, and they are growing sturdy, long roots instead of green shoots. So patience and wisdom are called for. If you are persisting in prayer and still feel "dry," consider that God may be growing something in your life that you're not aware of.

Am I respecting my own uniqueness? Your feelings, your thoughts and opinions, your individual temperament and abilities are all gifts from God. They are important tools to help you grow and should be treated with respect and gratitude. You don't have to live by your feelings, but you need to pay attention to them and accept that they are real. Living peacefully with others doesn't mean developing a different personality or never saying what you think.

The whole purpose of growth, after all, is to become the best possible version of who you are, not something entirely different. God would never expect a soybean plant to grow a beautiful ear of corn. Accepting God's gift of who you are is one of the best ways I know of to water your garden.

Am I aware of possible dangers that might hinder my growth? Even as an adult, you will not profit from repeated exposure to everything the world has to offer. As the apostle Paul pointed out, though all things are legal for believers, not all things are helpful (see 1 Corinthians 6:12). The Bible also warns us to watch over our hearts (Proverbs 4:23), and I think this is important for all of us to remember to be in our world but not of it (John 15:19). Repeated exposure to profanity, exploitive sexuality, or sensational news doesn't necessarily help us grow into the people God wants us to be. Neither do too many afternoons at the spa or the mall.

Guarding your heart from unwholesome influences just makes sense in this dangerous age. But keep in mind that God's primary call on our lives is not self-protection. If you spend all your time avoiding danger, you may well be stunting your growth instead of helping it. God is a dependable protector, after all, and he has specifically called us to carry his message out into the world. Prudence can be a wise choice in certain situations, but the choice to obey God and trust him for your protection is the wisest of all.

Am I trying to do too much alone? Your mentors, sisters, friends, family, and the body of Christ are all important resources God has given you for your growth. So are teachers and counselors. God has specifically promised the gift of his Holy Spirit for the process of our growth. Growing in Christ was never intended to be a Lone Ranger proposition.

And don't forget that the very process of living and working with others is part of the growing process. Working through communication problems with your husband helps you grow. Learning to cope with a domineering boss can help you grow. The challenge of teaching and training and loving your children makes growth almost inevitable.

In other words, don't fall into the trap of thinking you need to "get away" in order to grow. Yes, you need some time when you can withdraw into silence in order to process what has happened in your life, but you will probably do your best growing when you're intimately involved with others. And don't make the New Age mistake of thinking that growth is a "me, me, me" proposition. You can grow without sacrificing those you love on the altar of your own self-improvement.

Are you remembering to rejoice? This is the final and most important question to ask yourself. Living in this world is a great privilege, a precious gift from your Creator. Living as a follower of Christ, a redeemed saint, is an unbelievable privilege.

OTTO'S MOTTO

Don't run from.
Run to.

It's sort of a shame that many of us have to remind ourselves to rejoice, but it's easy to become distracted and bogged down when life gets messy. Gratitude is a learned skill—the antidote to distrust and despair. You can cultivate it in your life by consciously counting your blessings. Write them down in a special journal, or begin each entry in your regular journal with a list of five things for which you're thankful. (I did this every day for a year and was astonished by the change in my attitude over that time.) Develop a habit of thanking people who touch your life.

Make a point of celebration. Don't leave birthdays behind when children are no longer a part of your life. If no one thinks to throw someone a party, you do it. Develop a ritual for marking passages in your life. If old traditions lose their meaning, as sometimes happens, try something new.

If you feel bored or restless, focus on finding a pursuit that calls to you, excites you, energizes you. Ask God to help you find a place where you can serve with joy and energy, though you may need to complete current responsibilities before you give yourself fully to a new interest.

And in the midst of all this growing and changing, be sure to extend to yourself the same grace you extend to others. God does. He's always ready with a second chance, a new possibility, a surprising idea or opportunity.

At any season of your life, he's the God who makes all things new.

Even you.

A Moment of
REFLECTION

1. Write a paragraph describing how you see yourself at age 70. What changes might have to happen in your life in order for that vision to become a reality?

2. What circumstances in your life right now make you tend to resist the idea of growth?

3. What do you think is the secret to "guarding your heart" but also being salt and light in the world?

4. Think of a time in your adult life when you've done some of your most significant growing. What circumstances contributed to that growth?

HOW TO GROW—
A WHOLE-LIFE CHECKLIST

- You grow by practicing what you know to be right.

- You grow by stepping out in faith, even when you're not sure what to do.

- You grow by living in community and interacting with others.

- You grow by making mistakes and learning from them.

- You grow by reflection—not just "thinking about life" but examining yourself, thinking about where you are, and where you think you need to be.

- You grow by practicing time-honored disciplines of prayer, meditation, study, devotion, and fasting.

- You grow by listening to wise counsel.

- You grow by obeying God's Word and the call of the Holy Spirit.

- You grow by remembering where you've been...and moving forward.

TWENTY

THE GIFT
OF REPARENTING

THE WAY WE GROW IN OUR CHILDHOOD gardens has a huge influence on the person we become and the way we live our lives. Whether you find that good news or bad news depends on how you were raised. If you grew up in a warm, loving, Christian home with healthy, competent parents or guardians who were committed to your growth, your need for reparenting is at a minimum. But what do you do if you, like me, grew up in a less than ideal environment? What if your parents were abusive or neglectful or just ignorant? Or what if a divorce or death disrupted your childhood and prevented your parents from providing the kind of modeling and training and teaching and grace you needed to grow up physically, mentally, emotionally, and spiritually healthy?

The sad fact is that while God intends for all children to grow up in a healthy home, human sin often gets in the way. That's been true from the beginning of time, when Adam and Eve sacrificed their healthy home life for an afternoon snack. It's also been true since the beginning of time that sin tends to be passed down along family lines. Patterns learned in the home shape our growth in powerful ways. And the mistakes that parents make, even well-meaning ones, may well be repeated in the lives of children.

Unhealthy patterns such as addiction, abuse, and neglect can afflict generation after generation.

Does that mean you are doomed to repeat history in your own family, and that the painful circumstances that shaped you will ruin your children's lives as well?

Absolutely not.

The whole message of the gospel, after all, is that we don't have to be stuck in old patterns of sin. That applies to the generational sins that hold us back from growing just as it applies to the personal sin we've allowed to warp and misshape us. The reason I believe this so strongly is that I've experienced it. I've seen in happen in David's life as well, and in the lives of many other people I know. Faulty growth patterns *can* be changed. Mistakes *can* be redeemed. Negative behaviors learned in childhood *can* be transformed into positive ones. It's essentially a matter of claiming your full status as God's adopted child and letting him "reparent" you, replacing the negative growth patterns you learned in childhood with new, improved, positive ones.

How does reparenting begin? Like most significant change, it starts by recognizing there is a problem. Pride can make this an extremely hard thing to do. But if you grew up in a home that hindered your growth in some way, it's simply a fact that you may have a harder time growing and helping your children grow. Acknowledge that your negative childhood may have warped your attitudes and stunted your growth in ways you don't even recognize. You may have a hard time believing you are loved or may struggle with a sense that you are somehow inferior or damaged.

At the same time, the deficiencies in your background may give you an advantage—a deep desire to overcome your background and a deep passion for growth. I know that was true for David and me. We both grew up in households that were less than hospitable. My mother found entertaining guests an almost unbearable imposition. David's hardworking mother never enjoyed opening her home. But David and I each grew up with a deep hunger to establish a warm, welcoming household. Accomplishing this has been so important to us that we have been known to briefly leave our happy guests, hold each other close, and cry for joy at the sound of voices and laughter in our home. It's hard to say whether this desire to live hospitably came about in spite of our upbringing or because of it—probably both.

Regardless of the ways your less-than-ideal upbringing has marked you, an important next step is to specifically ask God to cover the sins that were done to you. Remind yourself daily that God is your real father, Christ is your brother, and you are surrounded by a great family of brothers and sisters in the body of Christ. When you said the Big Yes to Jesus, you opened your life to a process of being adopted and reparented by your heavenly Father.

Once you have committed the process of reparenting to the Lord, growing beyond the limits of your upbringing is a matter of trusting God to change your heart while you do everything you can to redirect your habits and thought processes. Because you grew up with inadequate or negative role models, it is especially important to study the Bible and the example of healthy families to get a clear picture of how a healthy home is supposed to work.

I urge you, especially if you are working to overcome a negative environment, to seek out a trusted older woman to act as a mentor, role model, and spiritual director. You, more than anyone else, need this kind of person in your life to help you reshape your attitudes and assumptions. Remember, however, that your mentor is a redeemed sinner like you—and she is not your parent. Learn from your mentor, but don't expect her to be perfect. And trust God to be your Father.

Being reparented in Christ is more than getting new role models. You will probably also need to train yourself in new, more healthy patterns of behavior. You may also need help in recognizing what behavior is unhealthy.

If addictions were part of your family experience, for instance, be aware that you may tend toward the same problems. You may have grown up hating your parent's alcoholism, for instance, and still learned patterns of addictive behavior. You may have also inherited a physical disposition toward addictions. It just makes sense, therefore, that you need to be especially careful in this area.

Raising your own children is another area that may require special attention. The fact is, no matter how much you hated the way you were parented, you'll still be prone to acting the same way with your children. I learned this truth to my own chagrin when Anissa came into my life, and I found myself resorting to the same rigid, overcontrolling parental tactics my mother had used on me. I was very hard on my little daughter—sometimes more concerned about being seen as a good parent than with actually *being* a good parent—and remembering that can still make me sad.

But I changed! It took time and a lot of work, but the change was real and profound. Once I became aware of what I was doing, I was able to make my parenting style a matter of specific prayer. I studied a whole library of good parenting books and watched the way Christian women I admired parented their children. I asked David and friends to hold me accountable for developing new ways of handling Anissa. Today, I think my daughter will still tell you I was a pretty strict parent, but not that I was a rigid, unreasonable one.

In all of this, keep reminding yourself that though you have been shaped by others' sin—as well as your own sin—you are not bound by these past sins. In Christ you are truly a new creation. With God's help you can break old patterns and grow in wonderful new directions.

Will it happen all at once? You know the answer to that. Will you make mistakes? They're a given. Will there be times when you repeat your parents' sins and dream up a few of your own? You can count on it. But you can also count on God's amazing grace and his dependable remedy for sin.

When you slip, confess to the Lord and accept his forgiveness. Confess and ask the forgiveness of those you have wronged, especially your children.

And finally, in obedience to Christ, I urge you to offer forgiveness to the parent or parents who wronged you. Although the pain is real, the hurt may not have been intentional. Acknowledge that he or she may well have been doing the best he or she could. And even if none of these things are true—if your growth was stunted by a malicious parent who actively disliked you and lived to cause you pain—realize that holding on to your resentment will only hold you back from future growth.

I happen to believe that true forgiveness and reconciliation cannot happen without repentance—that you cannot fully forgive a parent who will not or cannot admit what he or she has done. But even in cases where full forgiveness is not possible, it is still possible to open your heart to the possibility of forgiveness, to offer your ongoing pain and hurt to your heavenly Father, and move on.

No matter what life has done to you in the past, I urge you to accept that reality. No matter how barren or destructive or ugly your past, your place in the Father's watered garden is secure. Trust that. Rejoice in that. And let yourself "grow in the grace and knowledge of our Lord and Savior Jesus Christ. To Him be the glory, both now and to the day of eternity. Amen" (2 Peter 3:18).

A Moment of REFLECTION

1. What are some behaviors you learned from your family of origin that may be slowing your growth right now? Do you think you need to be "reparented" to overcome some of these problems?

2. What are some of the positive gifts you received from your family of origin? (Even the most negative background usually

contains *some* positives.) Can being grateful for these gifts help in the process of reparenting?

3. Does the idea of being reparented sound somehow disloyal to your own parents? How can you reject the negative aspects of your childhood without rejecting the people who raised you?

A Spirit
of Adoption

*N*o matter whether you grew up in a healthy, encouraging home or a place that stunted your growth, God looks on you as his child:

⊕ When the fullness of the time came, God sent forth His Son, born of a woman, born under the Law, so that He might redeem those who were under the Law, that we might receive the adoption as sons. Because you are sons, God has sent forth the Spirit of His Son into our hearts, crying, "Abba! Father!" Therefore you are no longer a slave, but a son; and if a son, then an heir through God (Galatians 4:4-7).

⊕ He predestined us to adoption as sons through Jesus Christ to Himself, according to the kind intention of His will (Ephesians 1:5).

PART FOUR

MAKING
YOUR HOME
A PLACE OF SERVICE

⌒♋⌒

*The King will answer and say to them, "Truly I say to you,
to the extent that you did it to one of these brothers of Mine,
even the least of them, you did it to Me."*

MATTHEW 25:40

TWENTY-ONE

YOUR MANSION IS YOUR MINISTRY

She was young, vibrant, and energetic. She loved the Lord, and she was devoted to her husband and new baby son. In fact, she had recently made the choice to be a stay-at-home mom, a choice that meant backing out of a number of volunteer positions she had once held in her church. Instead of devoting hours each week working with women's groups, my friend Terry now spent most of her time caring for the baby and her husband.

Her days were busy and full. Terry didn't regret her decision to stay home with her baby. But something was bothering her, and she confessed it to me one day.

"What I can't get used to," she said, "is not having a ministry."

I have to tell you, my heart broke just a little bit when Terry said that. This wonderful young woman was pouring her heart and soul into one of the most important and difficult jobs on this earth, investing her energies into raising a future saint—and she felt bad because she wasn't leading a Bible study?

Terry's problem was not a lack of ministry; it was a faulty understanding of ministry. And she's not the only one to fall for the fallacy that "ministry" is something that happens away from home—in the church, on the mission field, even at the office. Many people equate ministry with evangelism or outreach or church work—teaching Sunday school, running soup kitchens, organizing Christian conferences, helping youth groups build houses for the poor, going on mission trips, or perhaps visiting the sick in the hospital.

OTTO'S MOTTO

Your mansion *is* your ministry.

All these can be wonderful ways of serving—and that's what ministry essentially means: serving God and others. But these important activities aren't the *only* ways to serve. They're not even, necessarily, the most important. And limiting our view of ministry to such "out there" service can blind us to two important truths.

The first is that *if you are a follower of Christ, you have a ministry.* Period. You are called to love God with all your heart and soul and mind and strength, and to love your neighbor as yourself. You are called to live as salt in a flavorless world and as light to a world in darkness and to share the gospel with those who don't know it. And you are called to do all this *wherever* you find yourself—not just at church or on a mission trip, but at work, at the supermarket, and especially at home.

And this leads to the second truth, which is that *if God has given you a home, you have a home-based ministry.* Your home is holy ground, remember. How you live in your most intimate spaces and with your closest relationships matters deeply for the kingdom of God. It's part of God's plan to change your life and then through you to change the world.

It may be that your ministry efforts for a season or a lifetime may be focused within the four walls of your home. This is true for many of the young women I meet in Homemakers by Choice, who have chosen to be stay-at-home wives and mothers. It was certainly true for Terry, who, as I hastened to reassure her, *did* have a vital ministry, the ministry of motherhood. But even if you work outside the home or even if you invest your life in professional Christian service, your home is still holy ground. It's both a gift from God and a place where you are called to serve him.

It's so tempting to overlook or ignore this principle. It's part of our sinful human nature to discount or underestimate or just not see what is simplest and most basic—closest to home, so to speak. It's human nature to value the exciting or dramatic or highly visible over the mundane and familiar, to want to "save the world" while neglecting what is right under our noses.

Sometimes we become so focused on what is "out there" that we take for granted what is closest to us. Sometimes we may even feel that our home responsibilities get in the way of our ministry. And even if we don't feel that way, our culture may well presume to feel it for us—to remind us in both subtle and blatant ways that what happens outside our homes is what really matters.

But that is precisely Jesus' complaint against the religious authorities of his day—those whose primary interest was "ministry." Remember how he accused them of being "whitewashed tombs" full of corpses and corruption (Matthew 23:27)? Remember how he spoke of the priest and the scribe who went about their high-minded business while ignoring an injured and bleeding man at their feet (Luke 10:25-37)? Whatever else he was saying in these passages, he was also addressing the all-too-human tendency to concern ourselves with "out there" issues while ignoring what is closer to home.

Throughout the Bible, in fact, we can see that God typically does his transforming work from the inside out. He tends to work from the simple to the complex, from the particular to the general, from inner to outer, from small to large, from human hearts to individual families to chosen peoples and then to all the world.

- To create the human race, he started with a single man and woman—Adam and Eve.

- To renew the earth after the flood, he used a family—that of Noah.

- To set aside a people to bless the rest of the world, he began with Abraham and Sarah.

- To redeem humanity once and for all, he started with a baby in a manger—and, before that, a young girl who said yes.

- To spread the news of his kingdom, Jesus started with an inner circle of 12 whom he loved and trained for three years before sending them out into the world.

- To change the world after his resurrection, he sent his Spirit to a little group of terrified Christians.

And here's something interesting to consider: Jesus himself lived at home for 30 years, helping his parents and serving God, before beginning what we think of as his earthly ministry. Surely it's no accident that God calls us to begin our ministry from our own homes and our own nest.

Does he want us to reach beyond our homes to a world in need and have a wider ministry than within our families? Absolutely. He doesn't want our homes to be little fortresses that focus only on our well-being and keep others out any more than he wants us to be that way as individuals. But he has called us to a ministry that starts with the renewing of our own minds and the redemption of our souls and then radiates out from that center, beginning at home. Now, as always, God does the bulk of his transforming work from the inside out. In the heart. In individual lives. In the most intimate circles of human relationships. Which brings us back to our original point, which is that if God has given you a home, you have a ministry there.

You are called to serve Christ through your personal love and devotion, through prayer and reading the Word. You are also called to serve him by loving and caring for the people you encounter on a daily basis. Your husband. Your children. The neighbor who drops by to borrow a cup of sugar—or annoys you by letting her dogs "visit" your lawn. And from there, the world.

Chances are, of course, you are already serving others in your home. If you have children, that's guaranteed. But are you intentional about your ministry there? Do you consciously think of your home life as your ministry? Do you see what happens in your home as an important part of your service to the Lord? Are you living the words of 1 Corinthians 10:31, which urges us, "Whatever you do, do all to the glory of God"?

If you are like my young friend Terry, you may have fallen for the fallacy that your home life is one thing and your ministry is another. As a result, you may be working hard in the Lord's service and still feel like a second-class Christian citizen.

On the other hand, you may have fallen into the Pharisees' trap of polishing your more visible "outside" ministry and letting things slide at home. That's easy to do. It happens all the time. As I've said, it's human nature. I've done it too, which is why the words of my mentor Elisabeth Elliot hit me so hard so many years ago: "Don't carry a Bible unless you've swept under the bed."

So here's the truth to engrave on your heart as you live your life in this holy ground, your home: Your mansion is your ministry. It is holy ground, a sacred place, the inner circle where God wants to begin his transforming, redeeming work in your life and the life of others.

It's a matter of obedience, because the Bible tells us very specifically that we have a kingdom responsibility in our homes. For women, that responsibility includes living as helpers to our husbands, running our households responsibly, and helping influence the next generation for Christ.

It's also a matter of stewardship. God gives us homes as places of peace and safety, of rest and renewal, of love and growth. But our homes, like any other gifts, are intended for gratitude and sharing. Are you guilty of tithing your money but holding your gifts of home and family close to your chest?

Having said all that, then, I'd like to look at just a few specific ways that your mansion can be a place of ministry. The same old basic priorities hold. Your first place of ministry is to those things you alone can do.

You alone are responsible for your growth in Christ. In a sense, your first call of ministry is to grow in your own garden. You serve the Lord by reading his Word, by spending time with him in prayer, by worshiping him in your heart, and singing his praises in every room of your house.

If you are married, you alone can be a wife to your husband, so your first call is to minister to his needs—to love him, to be his helper, to support him in his walk with Christ. You serve the Lord by cooking your man's meals or ironing his shirts or speaking words of encouragement or not speaking words of discouragement. The details will vary according to your particular relationship, but the principle still holds. You serve the Lord by serving the man God has given you to love.

If you have children, only you can be mother to those children, so parenting is a vital part of your ministry. You serve the Lord by evangelizing them, modeling a godly life for them, teaching them, training them, helping them learn to live and grow in grace. More specifically, you serve the Lord by feeding them and wiping their bottoms and cuddling them at bedtime and insisting that they make their beds and say they're sorry. You serve the Lord by serving these little ones God has given you to love.

Your first call of ministry, then is *in* your home, to the people you love.

After that, I would suggest considering ways that God may be calling you to minister *with* your home—to open your living space and your life to others. This is essentially a ministry of hospitality. It encompasses much more than dinner parties, although I have seen great things happen for the Lord through dinner parties. You can minister with your home by allowing kids to gather there after school. You can host Bible studies and book clubs and let the neighbor kids hang out. You can open your home to an exchange student or a young person who needs a place to live while getting her finances in order.

Hospitality is essentially a form of stewardship. Our homes and apartments typically represent a large chunk of our income and the largest financial investment we ever make. Giving back some of that blessing in the form of a ministry of sharing is a natural response of duty and gratitude.

Beyond ministering in and with your home, you might finally want to consider ways that you and your family can reach out *from* your home to serve in your neighborhood, your community, and beyond. If you have children, especially, it is important that they learn to think beyond the narrow boundaries of themselves and their own needs, to see hurting people around them and hear God's call to minister to others. But I believe this process usually works best in the inside-out context, beginning with loving and serving at home, and then learning to reach out.

The thing to remember in all of this is that God is perfectly capable of arranging the circumstances of our lives to change the world. If we seek him first, he will show us where and how he wants us to serve. I have been absolutely amazed, over the years, at the places God has taken David and me. Who would ever have thought that I would travel to Ecuador and meet a sister in Christ who writes to me in Spanish on a regular basis? Who would ever have thought I would travel to Scotland and then, on a plane back, have the opportunity to connect a distraught mother of an anorexic daughter with the best treatment facility in my home state of Arizona? Who would ever have thought that I, a girl from a broken home, would found a ministry or write books about marriage and family that have reached women across the nation?

My point is, God is surprising. His ways are not our ways, and when we set out to follow him, he usually ends up leading us places we never thought we would go. But God's inside-out principle still holds. He calls you first to serve him in your heart, then in the inner circles of your relationships, and from there to a world in need.

What does that mean in practical terms? If you are running soup kitchens and singing in the choir at church and teaching community Bible studies while your home is a wreck and your family relationships are suffering, something's wrong. If you are working hard at home but somehow feel you're missing out on God's calling, something's wrong there too. If you are so busy either at home or in outside ministry that your inner life has gone parched and dry, something is definitely wrong.

But if you and those you live with are sharing love and serving one another, if your prayer life is strong and vital, if your home is a place of peace and lively growth, if you are opening your home and your heart in hospitality and reaching out from this strong center to serve a world in need, you are living just exactly as God planned for you to live.

Never underestimate the influence that your in-home ministry to those you love can have for the kingdom of God. I would suggest that this, in fact, is where the lion's share of God's work for the kingdom is done.

One home at a time, from the inside out.

A Moment of
REFLECTION

1. What does it mean to you specifically to have a home-based ministry? What does yours look like?

2. Can you think of times in your life where you fell into the trap of pursuing a ministry away from home while neglecting to serve those closest to you?

3. Can you think of times in your life when the opposite was true—when you were so involved with caring for your own that you failed to heed a call to reach out?

4. What, in your opinion, is the best way to strike a balance between empty outreach and ingrown ministry?

What Is My Ministry?

The foundation of ministry is character.

The nature of ministry is service.

The motive of ministry is love.

The measure of ministry is sacrifice.

The authority of ministry is submission.

The purpose of ministry is the glory of God.

The tools of ministry are the Word of God and prayer.

The privilege of ministry is growth.

The power of ministry is the Holy Spirit.

The model of ministry is Jesus Christ.

Author Unknown

TWENTY-TWO

YOU ALWAYS SERVE
THE ONES YOU LOVE

IF YOUR MINISTRY BEGINS IN THE HOME, what does a home-based ministry look like?

We've been describing it all through this book—we just haven't given it the name *ministry*.

You minister in your home by doing what you can to make it a place of rest and calm and order—setting the thermostat with your own loving and peaceful attitude, taking the time to organize and impose order, even decorating with rest in mind.

You minister in your home by making it a well-watered growing place for children and adults alike. You serve through your example, teaching, and training, and by the grace you show to those you love. You serve by being intentional about your own growth and doing whatever you can to help the people you live with grow in wisdom and stature and favor with God and man.

Some forms of home ministry are spelled out for us in the Bible. Wives are instructed to help their husbands and submit to them "as to the Lord" (Ephesians 5:22). Older women are to train younger women how to love and how to handle their households (Titus 2:3-5). Parents are to train their children and teach them about the Lord (Deuteronomy 4:5-10). All God's people are commanded to "encourage one another and build up one another"

(1 Thessalonians 5:11) and to "stimulate one another to love and good deeds" (Hebrews 10:24).

But beyond these basics are a wealth of opportunities for service within the walls of your home. God may well call you to any of a number of specific ministries that reflect your personal gifts, talents, and circumstances. They are also based on obedience to the Holy Spirit—responding to specific needs as the Spirit brings them to your attention.

Have you ever thought of your home as a place to exercise your spiritual gifts? Your spiritual gifts are really mine, you know; they are given for the benefit of me and everyone else in the body of Christ. If yours is a believing home, the people you live with are also part of the body of Christ, and your spiritual gifts are given to help you serve them as well. As you come to understand your gifts through prayer and the discernment of others in the body, discovering the gifts of wisdom or knowledge or faith or healing, remember that these gifts are for the building up of your "home body" first. Remember, too, that Paul's admonitions in 1 Corinthians 12 about using our spiritual gifts apply here—that these gifts are given as a means of helping others, not playing spiritual one-upmanship.

One of the most basic and important forms of service in the home is that of *practical help and support*. You serve your Lord and your family through your efforts to make your home a safe and comfortable environment. So many chores that fall under this heading—from scrubbing the toilet to cooking meals to reorganizing closets to waiting for the plumber—take on new significance when tackled intentionally as a form of loving ministry.

Never underestimate the power of a *prayer ministry* in your home. You serve both God and your family as you notice their needs and uphold them in prayer. Often, I find, my prayers for the people in my life lead to specific actions on their behalf. One of the most helpful habits I've developed in my own home is the using of my daily activities as cues for prayer. I've always prayed for David as I iron his shirts, for Anissa as I folded her clothes. I even pray for a certain young couple I love whenever I clean the lint filter of my dryer—because their own lint filter had sparked a significant conflict in their lives.

One of the most important ministries you can have in your home is a *ministry of encouragement*—supporting the people who share your home with uplifting and motivating words.

A *ministry of touch*, expressing affection and acceptance through your physical presence, can communicate to those you love in ways that words simply can't. When you kiss your husband, scratch your son's back, hug your mom, or swing your toddler around, you show love in a tangible way.

Have you ever thought you could have a *ministry of welcome* in your home—making it clear to those you love that you value their presence and enjoy their company? It's hard to underestimate the value of such a ministry in the life of a husband or child. One of the reasons people give for keeping dogs is that "they're always glad to see me." How much better is it to have a loving wife or mother or friend to greet you with a smile or a friendly word?

Can you have a *ministry of evangelism* within your home? If you have children, this is part of your mandate as a parent—to introduce your children to Jesus and help them understand their need for him and pray for their salvation. If your husband or someone else in your home is not a believer, your witness can be vital, but how you go about sharing the gospel can be a delicate matter. Certainly, you should pray and do your best to model a life of faith as lovingly and winsomely as possible. Certainly, you may try to be as open and honest about your beliefs as possible. But conducting a specific ministry of evangelism with an adult who is close to you may also mean disciplining yourself to back off and trust the Holy Spirit to work in the other person's life. The same human nature that makes us tend to overlook close-to-home ministry can make that ministry hard for our loved ones to hear. Living "unequally yoked" (being married to a nonbeliever) can be a lonely, difficult life—which is why the Bible counsels against choosing it. But living as a servant of Christ in such a situation can make a vital difference for the kingdom, which is why the Bible advises those who find themselves in such a situation to stay there and serve the best they can.

In addition to these basic ministries, God may call you to any of a number of specific ministries that reflect your personal gifts, talents, and circumstances. I have found it especially rewarding to study the way my household works and specific ways I can minister to my husband and daughter.

I have learned, for example, that in our home I have a *ministry of cheer*. I am the one who notices when David or Anissa is a little down, and I can almost always think of a way to make things better. My naturally cheerful disposition tends to brighten things up when they're gloomy, and my sensitivity to my family's moods enables me to be tactful rather than obnoxious about my good cheer. Over the years, as I've come to understand how this ministry works, it has brought me great joy. I love being the one who can adjust our emotional thermostat with my attitude. I love being able to serve my family in this way.

A very different form of ministry I've adopted in our household over the years is the *ministry of caring for my husband's shirts*. My husband is an attorney, and crisp, clean, perfectly starched shirts are a tool of that trade. Since the beginning of our life together, laundering and ironing his shirts on a weekly basis has been a labor of love for me. I'm perfectly aware that this makes me a bit of a dinosaur, and we could certainly afford to send the shirts to the laundry. But it has always meant a lot to David for me to do his shirts myself, and I love preparing them just the way he likes them. I love praying for my husband as I work on each shirt. I love knowing that each shirt is a pleasing gift of service to him.

Have I always enjoyed every minute of ironing David's shirts? Have I always felt happy and cheerful and excited about cheering up my daughter? Of course not. Ministry can be hard. Sometimes ministering to those we love is the hardest thing we'll ever do, and it's all the harder because our home ministries can be so easily ignored. When I find my motivation for home ministry flagging, I've found it helps to keep in mind a few truths about ministry.

First, keep in mind that being a servant to your husband and children is not the same as being a slave. When we serve others in the Lord, we are choosing to make sacrifices in obedience to God, not giving in to another person's power play. Our service is patterned after that of Christ, who *chose* to give up his rights and to minister to others out of love, not because he was manipulated or coerced. Serving others doesn't mean giving in to emotional manipulation or abuse. It doesn't mean giving in to every whine or waiting on children hand and foot. It means choosing to do what helps the people we live with—not because they force us to, but because we serve a Lord who loves them.

The second important thing to remember about your home-based ministry is that you have God's inexhaustible reservoir of strength and authority to draw from as a resource. The truth is, you will never possess enough human strength to minister to your husband, children, friends, and family the way that God directs. It is God who gives you the grace that is sufficient to every challenge of ministry.

OTTO'S MOTTO

If you've done it for one of the least of those you live with, you've done it for Me.

You need his love and grace to live sacrificially for others and to point them toward Jesus. You need his wisdom and guidance to make tricky choices—whether to work or stay home, whether to overlook a slight or confront an issue, whether to force your son to take another year of piano or require your daughter to work for her allowance. You need the Lord's authority to operate responsibly within your God-given roles—helping your husband, directing your children, witnessing to your friends and neighbors. For any ministry—especially in your home—you need the Lord.

At the same time, it's important to remember that the focus of all ministry is the Lord himself. Whether you're cooking, cleaning, touching, or encouraging the people you care about, what you're really doing is serving Christ.

Think of it this way. Imagine that you are meeting Jesus upon your entrance to heaven. He smiles warmly and says, "Welcome, blessed child of my Father. Come and enjoy the kingdom I have prepared for you. For I was hungry, and you went to the supermarket and stood in line at the checkout to buy me food, and then you brought it home and cooked it and served it with love. I was thirsty, and you went to the kitchen and fetched me a cold glass of water—without my even asking. I was feeling discouraged from a hard day at work, and you gave me a smile and a big hug and gave me some time to regroup. I had outgrown most of my clothes and the rest of them were dirty, but you still managed to find me something to wear. I was sick and you held my head as I threw up and then stayed up all night with me. I was holed up in my room, overwhelmed by my worry and insecurity, and you came to check up on me and make sure everything was all right."

"Wait a minute, Lord," you might interrupt. "I never went grocery shopping for you or gave you a hug or held your head while you were sick."

And he would reply, "Oh, yes you did. Whatever you did in loving ministry to the people in your life—on the holy ground of the home that I gave you—you did for Me" (see Matthew 25:34-40).

A Moment of
REFLECTION

1. What forms of ministry in your home bring you the greatest joy? Which do you find the hardest and most challenging?

2. What particular ministries have you forged in your home because of a particular need or gift? Can you think of any potential forms of ministry you could take on intentionally in the future?

Fresh Rather than Fried

God wants our homes to be centers for reaching to a hurting world. But I believe he also wants our homes to be places where we are refreshed and renewed for such service. Balancing these two purposes for our homes calls for much prayer and thoughtful decision making. Here are some suggestions that might help:

- Say yes selectively to outside ministry opportunities—and don't be afraid to say no. God wants you to serve, but he doesn't expect you to head every committee and host every Bible study.

- Give yourself and your family periodic time off for rest and re-evaluation. There's nothing wrong with claiming summers or Christmas as family time.

- During hectic seasons, consider short-term activities rather than long-term commitments. Instead of being "on call" to staff your church pantry, offer to work on a one-time basis or fill in for those who are sick. Instead of offering your home for a permanent Bible study, ask whether you could rotate locations.

- Periodically evaluate and adjust your outside commitments. Does what you are doing fit with your overall calling from God and your priorities? Have your circumstances changed? Are your outside ministry efforts shortchanging loved ones in any way?

- Don't let the time you spend doing for Jesus replace the time you spend with him.

TWENTY-THREE

A HEART
FOR HOSPITALITY

Be honest now.

When you think of inviting people into your home and entertaining them hospitably, don't you feel at least a little twinge of fear? Or nervousness? Or embarrassment? Does entertaining sound like a whole lot of work? Are you embarrassed to have other people see how you live? When people are coming to dinner, have you been tempted to go out and buy a new set of dishes and get your children to work scrubbing the baseboards?

If the young women I work with in the Homemakers by Choice organization are any indication, the very idea of hospitality can be daunting. But it doesn't have to be. Hospitality—opening your home and your life to friends and strangers alike—was never meant to be an overwhelming burden. God doesn't intend for any form of ministry to be like that. "My yoke is easy and My burden is light" (Matthew 11:30). I've found that's certainly true of hospitality. As with any form of service, it requires thought, energy, and lots of prayer. But hospitality that's done for the glory of God can be a truly joyful, liberating experience.

I actually learned my first lessons in hospitality from one of the least hospitable people I've ever met: my mother. She didn't mean to be inhospitable; she was just overwhelmed by the demands of her life and overloaded with her own expectations. But whatever her reasons, my mother hated having people in our house, even family. On those few occasions when she couldn't get out of hosting a family gathering, she made herself and everyone else miserable, including me. First she would drag out our one set of china dishes—they were kept in a box, a gift from an uncle who brought them back from Japan—and wash them. She would launder all the linens and scrub the house to the point of sterility. She would obsess about the food, although she was really not a very good cook and had little interest in the kitchen.

OTTO'S MOTTO

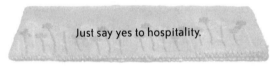

Just say yes to hospitality.

As a result of this frenzied preparation, of course, my mother was always exhausted by the time guests arrived. And she was never quite ready. When the doorbell rang, in fact, my mother was never there to greet her guests at the door because she was still in the bathtub. "Esther's still in the tub" became a family joke.

Even as a child, I knew there was something wrong with my mother's approach to hospitality. I knew it especially when I contrasted her attitude to that of other special women in our lives. My Aunt Pat, for instance, lived a very difficult life. Money was often extremely tight and relationships were often tense. Yet her home was always warm, always bright, always fragrant with the smell of something baking. I never entered her home without being offered something to eat or drink. I never visited without feeling that Aunt Pat was sincerely happy to see me and wanted me to be comfortable. At Aunt Pat's I felt like a beloved family member and an honored guest at the same time.

That's what I wanted—a home like that. David, who also grew up in a home where hospitality was a grudging chore, wanted that too. When we established our own household in our first house, we vowed we would have people in our home often and make them feel honored and welcome. From the earliest days of our marriage, we pledged ourselves to a ministry of hospitality.

Since then, we have hosted dinner parties, afternoon teas, after-church luncheons, swim parties, launch-of-ministry parties, picnics and potlucks, wedding and baby showers, and countless holiday gatherings, plus a wedding or two. (Most recently, we hosted a houseful of company for Anissa's wedding.) Babies, toddlers, tweens, and teens have attended gatherings at our home. So have elderly relatives and senior groups. New acquaintances and dear old friends have gathered around our table after church—often on the spur of the moment—or come over for an evening of Tripoly or cards.

Overnight visitors are a staple in our guest room—dear friends, visiting speakers, people in need of a bed for the night. From time to time we have even invited family members or young friends to live with us for months or even years at a time—definitely a stretching experience, but ultimately a fulfilling one. We have had the challenge and joy of providing a home for my sister-in-law and her children during a time of crisis in her life. We have cared for my mother and both of David's parents in our home. And from time to time we have provided living space for a young person who was trying to get her life together and in need of support and guidance. Each of these experiences has provided rich lessons in what it means to offer hospitality "as to the Lord."

Developing a ministry of hospitality in our home, in fact, has been one of the most exciting adventures of our lives together. But it didn't happen automatically—and it wasn't always easy. We didn't grow up with the best role models, remember, so we had a lot of learning to do. We suffered through our share of burned dinners, awkward moments, missed connections—plus a number of what David used to call my "pre-Thanksgiving twits," when the pressures of entertaining put me on overload and I made everyone around me miserable.

Making our home a place of true welcome has been a gradual, learn-as-you-go process, with both heartache and joy along the way. It has involved not only learning *how* to prepare for company and make people comfortable in our home, but also *what* true hospitality is and how God intended it to work. I had to learn that people would look at my happy face, feel my hugs, and wouldn't notice the quality of my carpet—that the work of serving others would fade in my memory, but the experience would be something I would cherish forever.

If you're experiencing twinges of dread at the thought of opening your home to others—or if you're prone to the occasional "pre-Thanksgiving twit" yourself—perhaps you can benefit from some of my experience.

One of the things that helped me most as I strove to create a hospitable home is to understand what hospitality is and what it isn't. In the first place, *hospitality isn't optional* for a follower of Christ. It isn't a spiritual gift given to some and not others, such as prophecy or teaching. Instead, it's a basic commandment, such as prayer or stewardship. It's a description of how all God's people are supposed to live all the time—with open hands and open hearts, welcoming strangers into our midst, opening our doors and our tables to those in need of a meal or a listening ear. It's an act of stewardship and obedience and worship. Even as God has given us a home and welcomed us into his family, even as Jesus has gone to prepare a place for us, we are required to welcome others into our lives and prepare a place for them as well.

All through the Bible, in fact, we find instructions and examples on living hospitably. In the book of Genesis, we have the story of Abraham offering hospitality to three strangers who turn out to be messengers of God (Genesis 18:1-8). Later, in Leviticus, God commands the Hebrews, "The stranger who resides with you shall be to you as the native among you, and you shall love him as yourself" (Leviticus 19:33-34). Hospitality to the needy was regarded as a dependable sign of true faith (Isaiah 58:6-9; Luke 14:12-14) and as a prerequisite for leadership in the early church (1 Timothy 3:2; Titus 1:7-8). Paul's bottom-line instructions to the Romans made it clear that "practicing hospitality" was a fundamental part of living as a Christian (Romans 12:10-13). And the book of Hebrews eloquently expands on this idea with an image that hearken back to Abraham's hospitality: "Do not neglect to show hospitality to strangers, for by this some have entertained angels without knowing it" (Hebrews 13:2).

To me, the best thing about knowing that hospitality is a divine command is remembering that God never tells us to do something without giving us the ability to do it. That means that when we make the effort to practice hospitality in God's name, we can expect the Holy Spirit to be present in our efforts. As we consciously open our homes and our lives to others, we make more room for the Spirit to work in us and those around us. Karen Mains' classic book *Open Heart, Open Home* inspired a generation of Christians to practice hospitality more intentionally, and she put it this way:

> Scripture teaches us that when we receive one another, we receive Christ; when we do for one another acts of tenderness, he is near. Loving reception only gives away what God has already given to us. I have learned to measure the success of my efforts at hospitality against the measurement of this question: "Did something sacred occur here in these rooms, around this table, in the moments of our meeting together?"*

"Something sacred"—isn't that a wonderful way to describe the ministry of hospitality? Thinking of it this way immediately highlights the differences between biblical hospitality and what our culture commonly calls "entertaining":

---

* Karen Mains, *Open Heart, Open Home: The Hospitable Way to Make Others Feel Welcome and Wanted*, rev. ed. (Downers Grove, IL: InterVarsity, 1976, 1997), p. 10.

Hospitality . . .	Entertainment . . .
Hospitality seeks to provide a *safe place*.	Entertainment seeks to provide a *showplace*.
Hospitality strives to *serve*.	Entertaining strives to *impress*.
Hospitality puts people before things.	Entertaining elevates things above people.
Hospitality claims that *what's mine is yours*.	Entertaining claims that *everything is mine* and you should admire it and certainly not touch it.
Hospitality *takes no thought for reward or reciprocation*.	Entertaining *expects praise and a return invitation*.
Hospitality is about *welcome, inclusion, and acceptance*.	Entertaining is about *exclusiveness and pride*.
Hospitality *frees us* to enjoy one another and grow in the Lord.	Entertaining *enslaves us* to personal and cultural expectations.
Hospitality specifically seeks out those in need of food, shelter, company, or a listening ear.	Entertaining seeks out those we think can help us in some way.
Hospitality is an act of obedience and stewardship.	Entertaining is essentially a self-serving occupation.

Can you see the difference? Your boss or your husband's boss or your friends at the country club may expect you to "entertain," but God doesn't. What God expects is for you to open your heart and your living space to make room for something sacred to happen. Hospitality, in other words, isn't a social obligation that we are expected to exchange with others. ("They invited us last month, so now we need to invite them.") It's not a performance in which we try to impress people with what we have and what we've done. ("And this is just a little thing we picked up on our last trip to the Orient.") And it isn't just for people we like or feel comfortable with or who can help us. In fact, the Bible is very specific that God is most pleased when we open our lives to those who are most in need and who have very few resources for returning the favor.

Does that mean that our guest lists should be made up entirely of men and women from the local homeless shelter? Certainly not. There are many different kinds of human need—for food and shelter, for friendship, for a listening ear, for a safe place or a little rest. When you think of it that way, "those in need" can include just about anyone we encounter in the course of our days. It certainly applies to a widow on a fixed income or the single mother who is one rent payment away from homelessness. But it can also apply to the annoying neighbor child who always seems to be hanging around and asking questions. It can apply to those in your household who come home craving a cheerful welcome or to an older relative who can no longer live alone. In fact, if you live in circles where "entertaining" really is obligatory, you might do well to consider that it is possible that a hospitable heart can transform even a social obligation into an act of grace. (Even bosses can be needy when it comes to hospitality.)

The most important thing to understand about hospitality is that it's something you *are*, not just something you do. Your ministry of hospitality starts with your eyes, your hands, and your heart. It's an attitude of welcome and acceptance that draws others in and makes them feel safe, honored, and loved. You can communicate hospitality to those in need even when you're not *in* your home.

OTTO'S MOTTO

Hospitality starts with your eyes,
your hands, and your heart.

I first saw this at work 30 years ago when my beloved Aunt Pat was in the hospital suffering from complications of diabetes. She was critically ill; in fact, she would never go home again. But even as my Aunt Pat lay dying in that hospital room, her hospitable spirit welcomed people into her life. Everyone around her felt it—the doctors, the nurses, the people who cleaned her room. When you entered Pat Sayad's room, you felt a welcome. She served others with her smile, her interest in their lives, her gratitude. Even in her last days, far from her home, her spirit of hospitality shone forth.

My Aunt Pat's example eloquently illustrated what the apostle Peter advised about the heart of hospitality: "Above all, keep fervent in your love for one another, because love covers a multitude of sins. Be hospitable to one another without complaint. As each one has received a special gift, employ it in serving one another as good stewards of the manifold grace of God" (1 Peter 4:8-10).

"Be hospitable...without complaint." Other translations specifically say "without grumbling"—an important word to those of use who are prone to the "pre-Thanksgiving twit." That kind of hospitality must be grounded in gratitude, infused with God's love, powered by the Spirit. If the idea of hospitality is a challenge to you, the first place to tackle it is on your knees.

Beyond that, here are some more practical suggestions that have helped me as I sought to make hospitality a part of our lives—to do it in a spirit of love, without grumbling and complaining.

First, it helps to be *intentional* about making hospitality a way of life. Hospitality thrives when you do it on purpose. Pray for opportunities to see needs around you and to extend hospitality to those who need it. Consciously invite the risen Lord to be both guest and host at all your gatherings. Plan for something sacred to happen every time you open your heart and your home to others—and be alert so you'll know when it happens.

Beyond that, just say yes to hospitality. Make it a way of life. You can short-circuit your fears and reservations by just diving in and learning to say "come in" and "come over." Make a point of suggesting "my house" for meetings, coffee klatches, work groups, or birthday celebrations. Push yourself to invite your neighbor in for a cup of tea, to ask your daughter's friend to stay for dinner, to take a turn at hosting your book club or Bible study.

This wasn't precisely what Paul meant by "practicing hospitality"—but it fits. The more you practice opening your home to others, the easier and more joyful it will be.

Saying yes to hospitality, of course, means saying no to excuses. You'll always be able to find an excuse for *not* practicing hospitality, but if you give in to the excuses you'll miss out on the blessing that comes with the ministry of hospitality.

You may say, "I don't have time." But with a little creativity I've found I can almost always squeeze in a little time for sharing. We all have to eat, for instance. Sharing cooking duties and a meal may actually take up less time than doing it all alone, or you can order takeout. If your time is really tight, look for ways to enjoy others while sharing the load. Some of my favorite times of fellowship have happened while helping a friend clean house or run a conference.

You may say, "I don't have the money." Early in our marriage, David and I used to host wonderful, hilarious, fulfilling evenings for less than a dollar. I'm not exaggerating. All it took was a 29-cent bag of popcorn, a five-cent package of Kool-Aid, a little oil for popping, some salt, a few board games or decks of cards, some people we cared about, and a willingness to give of ourselves. Granted, the cost of such an evening would be higher now—maybe as much as three dollars. But an evening of hospitable fun can still be a bargain. And by the way, offering hospitality on a tight budget is a great way to teach children to share. Dinner for four can become dinner for eight if everyone is willing to take a little less.

Another excuse: "I don't have the space." But I once hosted a birthday party with an international theme. Forty women answered my invitation, all in international costume. And at one point in the party I realized that all 40 women were gathered in our dining room around the table. Later I measured the space—all 40 women took up a space less than 15 by 18 feet. They weren't worried about space. They wanted to be together, to enjoy each other's fellowship.

Even if you are hosting overnight guests, space is probably not the issue you think it is. For me, having a designated guest room is a joy and a privilege, but we were in the habit of hosting overnight guests long before we had a separate room to put them in. We have been known to line up children in sleeping bags across our living room floor. We have given guests our bed while we slept on the living room sofa bed. We have also provided meals and company for guests who actually slept in motel rooms. With hospitality, as with any form of service, if your heart is in the right place you can find a way to serve.

Have you ever used this excuse? "My house is a mess, and I don't have time to clean it up." The long-term solution to that problem lies in changing some habits, and I have some suggestions for that below. But the short-term solution is to swallow your pride, move the magazines off the chairs, dig through the cluttered pantry for some chips and salsa, and welcome your guests as warmly as you can. I'll never forget the woman who taught me that hospitality trumps cleanliness. Her house was almost always in disarray, but her welcome and her coffeepot were always warm, and I loved spending time with her—even with laundry piled beside me on the sofa.

All these excuses, of course, represent something to keep in mind when planning for hospitality. If funds are tight, you probably don't want to serve caviar. If space is limited, you may want to plan a series of small gatherings rather than a large party. If you have no yard or patio, a spaghetti dinner might work better than a barbecue. If your house is always a mess, consider how you could keep things in better order—and let your desire to be hospitable be a motivation. And if your house is being remodeled, you may choose to move the whole shebang to a shelter in a local park or your church fellowship hall. But watch out for reasons that are really excuses. Say yes to hospitality, practice it whenever you can, and ask God to help you learn from it what it means to live a life of welcome.

You can make this whole process a lot easier if you abandon your double standard when it comes to cleanliness, maintenance, and order. Instead, make it your goal to develop the same—reasonable—standards for both family and guests. That way, your family will enjoy the benefits of a more pleasant environment and you'll (almost) always be ready to extend hospitality without undue anxiety.

OTTO'S MOTTO

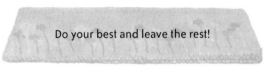

Do your best and leave the rest!

Here's an example. I used to clean and polish our dining room chandelier before every dinner party. Maybe you think that's obsessive, and you may be right—I was raised by a woman who washed the top of the refrigerator every day! Today, however, I have a schedule in which I clean the chandelier once a month and polish it twice a year—no matter who is in the house. You may prefer to polish your chandelier every week, or settle for an annual dusting, or just remove the thing altogether and install track lighting. The point is to treat your family like guests and your guests like family—and to spare everybody that last-minute drive to make everything perfect. (The same principle applies, by the way, to "company manners." The basic rules of courtesy should apply to living together as a family as they do to having guests.)

Does this mean you should never do anything special or out of the ordinary when company comes to call? I hope not, because I love planning special celebrations and serving my guests in memorable ways! I love putting together elaborate skits, entertaining programs, intriguing questions. I love dreaming up creative ways to help my guests know each other better. To me, that's part of the joy, and it's also a way to show guests that you value them enough to spend time on them. When you open your home to special gatherings, by all means take the time to decorate, to prepare fun foods, to dream up special activities and wear special clothes. Just make sure to allow enough time to get everything done, keep your expectations in check, and keep your fussing and fuming to a minimum to make the practice of hospitality easier and more pleasant for everyone involved. It really is possible to open your home to guests without throwing a fit ahead of time.

Actually, a little general planning can help a lot in cutting down on pre-event stress and making hospitality a way of life in your home. You can simplify your life tremendously by keeping your home—and your heart—prepared for hospitality at any given moment. This includes not only keeping the house relatively clean and organized, but also stocking the pantry and the refrigerator. In my house, for instance, I always like to have a covered cake dish with something fresh baked in it. I keep my refrigerator stocked with juices and colas and the pantry stocked with coffee and tea. I keep bottled water on hand because I know young people like bottled water, even though I personally dislike the idea of having to buy water. I also have developed several menus I can throw together at the last minute using canned food, frozen goods, and whatever fresh produce I might have on hand. Over the years, I have even gradually invested in a variety of outdoor tables, chairs, and umbrellas so I can serve people outdoors—a favorite Arizona activity—without the chore of lugging furniture outside.

I try to keep my attitude hospitality-ready too. This can be a distinct challenge when I am in one of my focused, get-my-work-done modes. I don't really like to stop what I'm doing to offer unplanned hospitality. But I am learning to be a little more open to God's interruptions, a little more ready to entertain angels when they arrive in my life. When I manage this kind of flexible hospitality, I am almost always the richer for it. In fact, I find that such spur-of-the-moment opportunities for hospitality are almost always potential blessings.

When you're anticipating a particular gathering or event, of course, you'll have to do more specific planning. You'll need to consider the purpose of the evening, your guests' specific needs, and ways you can make the evening run smoother. By all means, think ahead about table settings, menus, and activities. Brainstorm every possible way you can to make your guests feel honored and loved. Do whatever you can to make the evening a happy and memorable experience for everyone involved. Prepare so that guests are never in doubt that you have eagerly anticipated their arrival. Taking the time to plan, to organize, and get things done ahead of time will almost always make you a more confident, calm hostess and help your guests feel honored. So make lists and seating charts. Set the table or hang streamers or blow up balloons the day before. Arrange food in serving dishes and refrigerate them ahead of time.

But even while you're planning and preparing, keep in mind my mother's bathtub hospitality and my pre-Thanksgiving twits! Think about Jesus' friend Martha, who almost ruined a dinner with her Lord by being "worried and bothered about so many things" (Luke 10:41). Think about Peter's reminder that we're supposed to serve others "without complaint." It's important to prepare, in other words, but *overpreparation* can lead to family discord and a frazzled spirit. I would guess that more evenings have been ruined by a stressed-out hostess than by a lack of preparation—and the same stressed-out hostess may have soured her family on the very idea of entertaining! You can avoid your own pre-whatever twit by making serenity of spirit one of your hospitality goals.

Serenity comes more easily, of course, when you keep things simple. As I've already shown, hospitality doesn't need to be expensive or elaborate. All you really need to offer hospitality is a glass of water or cup of tea, a chair, and a smile. Even beyond that, a few basics will suffice. For dinner parties, I've gotten amazing mileage out of a set of white dishes and a few menus I can make in my sleep. I've served the same spaghetti dinner (with an apron on every chair) or Sunday pot roast to countless groups of friends— with an "elegant" dessert of Jell-O whipped with ice cream and served in stemmed glasses with fresh strawberries. And not a single one has ever complained because what I served wasn't fancy enough. The experience of being included and welcomed was what my guests remembered.

Over the years, of course, as my confidence and bank account grew, I have learned how to expand on the basics. With careful planning and enough lead time, I've learned that hosting a small dinner party and hosting a crowd are not all that different. I love dishes, so my collection of china and pottery has expanded. I like to cook, so I've expanded my "old faithful" menus and even tried out new recipes on company. (They usually enjoy being included in the experiment.) I've acquired a collection of table linens, all variations on my signature color scheme of black and white, and I've also had fun experimenting with seasonal decorations.

But these are all fun extras, not hospitality essentials. And the basics of hospitality still apply: something to eat and drink, something to do, a welcoming spirit.

Serenity, too, comes from making comfort a priority. You want to make your guests comfortable, of course. But to do that, you need to make yourself comfortable too. Wear clothing that suits what you will be doing. That stunning white lacy blouse might not be the best choice for serving a spaghetti dinner. And remove any objects you fear might be damaged or pose a danger so you won't have to spend your time worrying about them. This is especially important if children will be your guests. You don't need to completely childproof your house for a short visit, but you'll all be more comfortable if you help them succeed at being good visitors. A friend of mine used to bring her small boys over to visit, and we would enjoy strawberries and chocolate dip on plastic tablecloths on the floor. We all had fun at these informal picnics, the cleanup was a snap, and the boys didn't have to worry about keeping everything clean.

Finally, for the richest experience of hospitality, try to involve everybody as fully as possible. If you have children, let them help with planning events and preparing for guests—and make sure they're part of cleanup as well. Your ministry of hospitality becomes a training tool as you teach children to greet guests at the door, to take coats and put them away, to speak politely with adults, and put their guests' needs above their owns. (Don't forget to help them show hospitality to their friends too.)

There's nothing wrong with asking your guests to pitch in as well, especially for an informal gathering. You don't invite people into your life to do your work for you, but there's a warm welcome implied by letting guests be part of the family. Because I am a planner by nature, I've even learned to plan ways for guests to help. I always like to have an answer ready for "what can I do?" Whatever I can do to make a guest feel accepted and included and honored and loved, I want to include in my hospitality efforts— because I have learned that such efforts please God, and because sharing my life and my home brings me such joy.

Often, in the midst of one of our gatherings, with the lively sounds of friends and family in the background, David and I will sneak off into a quiet corner and listen to the sounds of laughter and fellowship. Our ministry of hospitality is something we've worked hard to develop, but it's also something we cherish and are always ready to celebrate.

We'd love you to join us.

Are you ready to say yes?

A Moment of
REFLECTION

1. Is hospitality a ministry that comes easy to you? If not, what excuses stand in the way of being more hospitable?

2. What role models can you copy as you strive to live more hospitably?

3. Just do it. This Sunday after church, vow to bring someone home with you to dinner. For a real challenge, do it without spending all day Saturday cleaning the house!

Mi Casa Es Su Casa:
GUIDELINES FOR HOSTING GUESTS OVERNIGHT

Having people in your home overnight can be a blessing, a challenge, and a true ministry. Here are some ideas for keeping things pleasant and meaningful:

- *Prepare a place for your guests. It doesn't need to be fancy, but aim for a modicum of privacy.*

- *Be sensitive about meeting your guests' particular needs. Will they need a reading light, extra shampoo, an alarm clock, a hair dryer?*

- *Share what you have. Make "your house is my house" a theme of every visit. Be sure your guests know what to do if they get hungry or thirsty and you're not around.*

- *Give your guests an idea of how the household normally works— when you get up, when you go to bed, when the children can be expected to get loud, and so on. Make sure they know where they're going to sleep, where the bathroom is—and that the loud "whoosh" in the middle of the night is merely a plumbing idiosyncrasy.*

- *Include your guest in regular home activities—even chores, if they want to help. But for short visits, try to spend most of your time on being together.*

REACHING OUT

IN THE END, YOU KNOW, it's all about Jesus.

The ministry of our homes, the way we live together, the way we organize and show our love and grow—it's all about Jesus.

When we serve our loved ones in our homes, it's about him. We do it out of gratitude for what he has given us. We do it out of obedience, because he has commanded us. We do it as a form of service to him who loves our families more than we ever could.

When we open our hearts and lives in a ministry of hospitality, that's about Jesus too. We welcome others because he has welcomed us. We take pains to prepare for guests because he has taken such infinite pains to prepare a place for us. We expect something sacred to happen in our gatherings because he has brought us together for a sacred purpose—to bring out his heavenly kingdom both here on earth and throughout eternity.

In the end, the Lord is what all our ministry is about or it's not about anything at all. Our homes are holy ground because it is there that we encounter his countercultural calm, his transforming growth, his serving sacrifice in its most intimate form. What happens here is both so huge and yet so comfortingly small that our best response is to take off our shoes in both awe and relaxation. When

Christ lives in our homes and our lives as both host and guest, something sacred just has to happen.

But our lives, of course, are not lived out entirely at home, and Christ's transforming presence is bigger and wider than our four walls could ever hold. Our homes are vital starting places, the place where we live out kingdom values on the most personal level. They are to be treasured for the gift they are, nurtured and stewarded for God's glory. How we live there matters. The choices we make matters.

But we were never supposed to live our lives huddled within those four walls, minding our own business and congratulating ourselves on how God has blessed us. That's the other side of God's inside-out approach to changing the world. Even when our lives are centered at home, our eyes and our hearts are to be focused outward, on a world in need of a Savior.

Just as God chose the people of Israel to be a blessing to the entire world, he wants our families to be a blessing too. A blessing to our extended families, to our neighbors, to the local body of Christ with whom we share and worship. A blessing to our communities, our nation, and to the world. A blessing to those who only know life as popular culture explains it, or as their particular history has shown it to them. A blessing to those who are starving for the truth we—hopefully—encounter and live in our homes.

Your mansion really is your ministry, in other words, but it's a ministry meant to benefit all humankind. And *that* should really motivate you to take off your shoes, because as mundane as your daily life can be, it's one of God's most important tools for redeeming the world.

How does it happen?

It happens as we live out our countercultural calm and transforming love, showing those around us that God's peace is deeper and more satisfying than anything the world can give.

This happens as we grow together in grace, preparing godly children and adults who have the strength and integrity to buck the trends and intentionally live God's way.

And it happens as we reach out in ministry, serving first in our most intimate circles, reaching out from there to include strangers and the needy in a ministry of hospitality, and finally, if and when God leads, pouring out our lives in ministry outside our homes. It happens when we turn our focus outward and intentionally dedicate our home lives to the purposes of the gospel.

Once again, this doesn't mean we are to neglect our close-to-home ministries. If things aren't working well at home—if relationships need healing or children need attention—that's probably a sign that outside ministries can wait. If we aren't tending to our top priorities, we can hardly expect the Lord to bless our efforts at outreach.

But if your home is thriving, if you are learning to live together in peace and give God's kind of love away and grow in healthy directions, the natural next step is to reach out and share what is happening in your home.

What exactly should you do? I suggest you start in your immediate neighborhood. Look around you and ask the Holy Spirit to point out opportunities for ministry. Ask him to show you who is hungry and thirsty and naked and in prison—whether literally or not. Ask him to point out ways you can meet those needs.

OTTO'S MOTTO

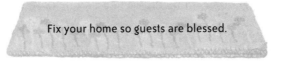

Fix your home so guests are blessed.

Another place to start is in your church. What ministries can you plug into? What areas of God's work in that particular body could benefit from your help? Be sure and pray about this as well and seek the Spirit's guidance. Choosing an avenue of ministry is not just a matter of picking something that sounds fun or interesting. It's a matter of finding your fit, locating a ministry where you can do the most to further the kingdom.

And although you may find much to do as an individual, why not look for ways to serve together with those who share your home? Look for ways you can reach out as a family and, in the process, strengthen the bonds of love that keep you together.

Your inside-out family ministry may be as simple as baking cookies and taking them to a shut-in (nondiabetic!) neighbor.

It may be as complex as agreeing to taking in a foster child (as friends of ours have done) for a year or taking three months to minister together as a family on a hospital ship.

Your ministry may be as practical as volunteering for your family to be greeters or offering takers in church on Sunday morning—or as exciting as starting a family band and playing for revivals and conferences.

It may be as ordinary and as life-changing as making friends and having those friends in your home and gradually helping them come to know the Savior.

How can you choose what forms of outreach are best for you? Here are just a few considerations:

- What particular combinations of gifts does our family have for ministry?

- What have we done well together in the past?

- What kinds of things do we like to do?

- Is God calling us to a particular ministry—and does he want us to serve individually or together?

- Does one person in our family have a heart for a particular kind of outreach that could become a family project?

- What kinds of activities will teach our children best about what God expects of us in ministry and also how he blesses our efforts?

In our own home, David and I have found that our outreach efforts have grown naturally out of our areas of interest and expertise. For instance, my experience as a homemaker, my passion for mentoring, and my interest in home organization led me to found the "mentors and moms" organization that grew into Homemakers by Choice. My husband's legal and financial skills and his pastoral heart helped us develop a sideline ministry counseling young couples in the spiritual, emotional, practical, and financial aspects of marriage.

Finding an appropriate outside ministry—and doing it—is an everyday, up-and-down process, just like life at home. Flashes of insight and meaning may only occasionally interrupt long spells of plain old work. Ministry, like family living itself, involves imperfect people who mess up on a regular basis, who must backtrack and repent and ask forgiveness and try again. It requires multiple slatherings of grace—heaped higher and higher, covering a multitude of sins.

But when it's working right, and when you're seeing straight, your ministry shows itself for what it is—a life infused with other-worldly loveliness. With the life-changing presence of the living Christ.

So I invite you, as you finish this book, to take off your shoes. Look around you, and the home the Lord has given you, and open your eyes to its holy possibilities. Your essential purpose as a mom—and also as a wife, mother, daughter, and friend—is to use the blessing of your home to bless others and to bring about the kingdom of God. Your task is to say yes to what God wants to do in your life and in your home and to proclaim, in the process, that you are blessed among women.

In the process, you'll be serving the Lord—you and all your house.

Thanks for letting me visit your home.

Ideas for Family Ministry

*A*lways be on the lookout for ways your whole family can reach out to a hurting world. Here are just a few ideas:

- ☙ Share a meal. *The next time your children spot a homeless person on the street, drive to a nearby restaurant, purchase a meal to go, tuck in some coupons and a little cash, and drive back by. (It's all right to discuss some of the hard questions about giving handouts—just don't let that become a cynical excuse for never helping.)*

- ☙ Pray together. *If your church keeps a prayer list, post it on the refrigerator or the kitchen table. Talk together about the needs represented there. Pray together as a family. If appropriate, find a way to help—visiting the hospital, delivering a pot of soup, or just sending a note or card. (A shut-in would probably love receiving a handmade card from your five-year-old.)*

- ☙ Practice random acts of kindness as a family. *One possibility: Buy bouquets or plants in the grocery store and give them to someone who looks as though they could use a lift.*

- ☙ Run together. *Participate in a walk or fun-run for a godly cause such as fighting hunger.*

☙ Host a happening. *Hold your women's groups or Bible studies in your home so your children can have an inkling of what goes on when God's people pray and share and study together. For practice in ministry and manners, why not have your children prepare and serve the refreshments?*

⤬

ADDITIONAL RESOURCES

Cheapskate Monthly
(www.cheapskatemonthly.com)

Founder: Mary Hunt
Address: P.O. Box 2135, Paramount, CA
90723-8135
Phone: (562) 630-6474
Fax: (562) 630-3433

Crown Financial Ministries
(www.crown.org)

Founder: Larry Burkett
Address: P.O. Box 100, Gainesville, GA
30503-0100
Phone: (770) 534-1000

Family Matters
(www.TimKimmel.com)

Address: 13402 N. Scottsdale Rd., Suite
A120, Scottsdale, AZ 85254
Phone: (480) 948-2545

Hearts at Home
(www.hearts-at-home.org)

Founder: Jill Savage
Address: 900 W. College Avenue, Normal,
IL 61761
Phone: (309) 888-MOMS
Fax: (309) 888-4525

Miserly Moms
(www.miserlymoms.com)

Founder: Jonni McCoy
Address: P.O. Box 49182, Colorado Springs,
CO 80949

Moms in Touch International
(www.momsintouch.org)

Founder: Fern Nichols
Address: P.O. Box 1120, Poway, CA 92074-
1120
Phone: (800) 949-MOMS

Mothers at Home
(www.mah.org)

Founder: Janet Dittmer, Cheri Loveless and
Linda Burton
Address: 9493-C Silver King Ct., Fairfax,
VA 22031
Phone: (800) 783-4666

Mothers of Preschoolers
(www.mops.org)

Founder: Elisa Morgan
Address: P.O. Box 10220, Denver, CO
80250-2200
Phone: (800) 929-1287 or (303) 733-5353

Proverbs 31 Ministry
(www.proverbs31.org)

Founder: Sharon Jaynes
Address: P.O. Box 17155, Charlotte, NC
28227
Phone: (877) P31-HOME

How to Contact the Author

For more information on Donna Otto's ministry or to communicate with
Donna about speaking engagements, please contact her at:

www.donnaotto.org or *www.HomemakersByChoice.com*
or
Donna Otto
11453 North 53rd Place
Scottsdale, AZ 85254
480-991-7464

Other Books
by Donna Otto

GET MORE DONE IN LESS TIME

Transform a hopeless schedule into a healthy lifestyle with room to breathe! Readers will discover easy ways to save steps in the kitchen, streamline shopping, create joyful holiday gatherings, use their planners effectively, and more.

THE STAY-AT-HOME MOM

This expanded and revised guide offers up–to–date information for mothers at home and those who want to be. Otto, with boundless enthusiasm for home and personal organization, takes on the challenges and highlights the rewards of being a stay–at–home mom.

FINDING A MENTOR, BEING A MENTOR

Helping women share the joys and pains of everyday life, mentoring provides a venue for discussing effective strategies for navigating the demands of being a wife, mother, friend, and businesswoman.

HARVEST HOUSE
PUBLISHERS

Other Good Harvest House Reading

THE POWER OF A PRAYING® PARENT
by *Stormie Omartian*

Popular author and singer Stormie Omartian offers 30 easy-to-read chapters that focus on specific areas of prayers for parents. This personal, practical guide leads the way to enriched, strong prayer lives for parents.

365 THINGS EVERY NEW MOM SHOULD KNOW
by *Linda Danis*

This daily guide to the first year of motherhood combines prayerful, playful, and practical information to energize new moms. Features weekly devotionals and daily activities that foster a baby's physical, emotional, social, and spiritual growth.

THE MOTHER LOAD
by *Mary M. Byers*

Motherhood is an intense, 'round-the-clock job. To stay healthy and happy, moms need friends, laughter, solitude, balance, and an intimate relationship with the Lord. *The Mother Load* offers down-to-earth suggestions, spiritual truths, and real-life advice from moms to help women survive and thrive in today's active families.

A MOM AFTER GOD'S OWN HEART
by *Elizabeth George*

Elizabeth George's *A Mother After God's Own Heart* offers 10 principles to help moms make God an everyday part of their children's lives. Elizabeth, who has two grown children and six grandchildren, gives practical advice and real–life suggestions for helping children—no matter what their ages—incorporate God into daily life.

HARVEST HOUSE
PUBLISHERS